4th Watch Books™

Forward

Our purpose for publishing the documents issued by the National Institute of Standards and Technology (NIST) is twofold. First of all, each NIST title in and of itself is very informative, however I am of the opinion that they should be looked at from the standpoint that each title is an integral part of a holistic cybersecurity strategy. Rather than look at each title just by itself, we need to look at them in groups based on how they are interrelated and designed to work together to improve cybersecurity.

For example, this particular group on PRIVACY SECURITY includes the following titles:

NIST SP 800-53 R 4   Security and Privacy Controls for Federal Information Systems and Organizations

NIST SP 800-53A R 4   Assessing Security and Privacy Controls

NIST SP 800-122   Guide to Protecting the Confidentiality of Personally Identifiable Information (PII)

NIST SP 800-188   De-Identifying Government Datasets - (2nd DRAFT)

NISTIR 8053   De-Identification of Personal Information

NISTIR 8062   Introduction to Privacy Engineering and Risk Management in Federal Systems

In order to assemble the entire picture of privacy security – from what it is, how it works, what the vulnerabilities are, and how to mitigate them, one must assemble all of these documents. Only by going through all of them can a person understand the complete picture. Leave one of them out and you would be missing a valuable piece of the privacy security puzzle.

Why buy a book you can download for free?

That brings me to the second reason to publish the NIST standards and that is the logistics of it all. These 7 publications consist of 771 pages. That's enough paper to fill two large three-ring binders. Nobody has a secretary anymore, so an engineer that is paid $75 an hour has to do this. The amount of time it would take an engineer to print all 7 publications (using a network printer shared with 100 other people – and it's out of paper, and the toner is low), punch holes in 771 pages and assemble the binders would easily take half a day.

Our ability to deliver any NIST document quickly and efficiently is unmatched because we are printing books on demand and we are backed up by Amazon, so the titles are easy to find and simple to order. Just search Amazon.com by NIST number and you can have a copy shipped to you in a matter of days. We print all books a full 8 ½ inches by 11 inches, with large text. If there are color images in the publication, the book is probably in color, unless the color is merely decorative, in which case we print in black and white to keep the cost to you as low as possible.

Luis Ayala,
My email is cybah@webplus.net   Our website is: cybah.webplus.net
4th Watch Books is a Service Disabled Veteran Owned Small Business (SDVOSB).

NISTIR 8062

An Introduction to Privacy Engineering and Risk Management in Federal Systems

Sean Brooks
Michael Garcia
Naomi Lefkovitz
Suzanne Lightman
Ellen Nadeau

This publication is available free of charge from:
https://doi.org/10.6028/NIST.IR.8062

National Institute of
Standards and Technology
U.S. Department of Commerce

NISTIR 8062

An Introduction to Privacy Engineering and Risk Management in Federal Systems

Sean Brooks
Michael Garcia
Naomi Lefkovitz
Suzanne Lightman
Ellen Nadeau
Information Technology Laboratory

This publication is available free of charge from:
https://doi.org/10.6028/NIST.IR.8062

January 2017

U.S. Department of Commerce
Penny Pritzker, Secretary

National Institute of Standards and Technology
Willie May, Under Secretary of Commerce for Standards and Technology and Director

National Institute of Standards and Technology Internal Report 8062
49 pages (January 2017)

This publication is available free of charge from:
https://doi.org/10.6028/NIST.IR.8062

Comments on this publication may be submitted to: privacyeng@nist.gov

National Institute of Standards and Technology
Attn: Applied Cybersecurity Division, Information Technology Laboratory
100 Bureau Drive (Mail Stop 2000) Gaithersburg, MD 20899-2000
Email: privacyeng@nist.gov

All comments are subject to release under the Freedom of Information Act (FOIA).

Reports on Computer Systems Technology

The Information Technology Laboratory (ITL) at the National Institute of Standards and Technology (NIST) promotes the U.S. economy and public welfare by providing technical leadership for the Nation's measurement and standards infrastructure. ITL develops tests, test methods, reference data, proof of concept implementations, and technical analyses to advance the development and productive use of information technology. ITL's responsibilities include the development of management, administrative, technical, and physical standards and guidelines for the cost-effective security and privacy of other than national security-related information in federal systems.

Abstract

This document provides an introduction to the concepts of privacy engineering and risk management for federal systems. These concepts establish the basis for a common vocabulary to facilitate better understanding and communication of privacy risk within federal systems, and the effective implementation of privacy principles. This publication introduces two key components to support the application of privacy engineering and risk management: privacy engineering objectives and a privacy risk model.

Keywords

Computer security; cybersecurity; information security; privacy; risk management; systems engineering

Acknowledgements

The authors wish to thank the following individuals for participating in the preparation of this document: Jeremy Berkowitz, James Dever, Simson Garfinkel, Meredith Jankowski, and Colin Soutar. They'd also like to recognize Kelley Dempsey, Marc Groman, Mat Heyman, Kat Megas, Rebecca Richards, and Ron Ross for their role in the review process. The authors are particularly grateful to Simson Garfinkel, who was so generous with his time and thoughtful feedback. A special note of thanks goes to Kaitlin Boeckl, who developed the graphics found herein. And finally, in developing the privacy risk model, the authors greatly appreciate the insights from the pilot programs funded by NIST pursuant to the National Strategy for Trusted Identities in Cyberspace (NSTIC).

Executive Summary

NIST research in information technology—including cybersecurity, cloud computing, big data, and the Smart Grid and other cyber-physical systems—aims to improve the innovation and competitiveness that bring great advancements to U.S. national and economic security and quality of life. Much of this research pertains to the trustworthiness of these information technologies and the systems in which they are incorporated. Given concerns about how information technologies may affect privacy at individual and societal levels, the purpose of this publication is to provide an introduction to how systems engineering and risk management could be used to develop more trustworthy systems that include privacy as an integral attribute.

In addition, the Office of Management and Budget's recent update to Circular No. A-130 includes a new emphasis on managing privacy risk. Federal agencies will need guidance on repeatable and measurable approaches to bridge the distance between privacy principles and their effective implementation in systems.

Extensive guidance already exists for information security. In developing an engineering approach to privacy, it is important to understand the relationship—and particularly the distinctions—between information security and privacy. Doing so will improve understanding of how to apply established systems engineering and risk management processes to addressing privacy concerns. Although unauthorized access to personally identifiable information (PII) is a subset of information security and a critical aspect of privacy, there is a far less developed understanding of how to identify and address the risks to individuals' privacy that extend beyond unauthorized access to PII.

For purposes of this publication, privacy engineering means a specialty discipline of systems engineering focused on achieving freedom from conditions that can create problems for individuals with unacceptable consequences that arise from the system as it processes PII. This definition provides a frame of reference for identifying a privacy-positive outcome for federal systems and a basis for privacy risk analysis that has been lacking in the privacy field.

To support agencies' ability to conduct privacy engineering, this publication introduces a set of privacy engineering objectives—predictability, manageability, and disassociability—to help system engineers focus on the types of capabilities the system needs in order to demonstrate how an agency's privacy policies and system privacy requirements have been implemented. In addition, this report introduces a privacy risk model to enable agencies to conduct more consistent privacy risk assessments based on the likelihood that an operation performed by a system would create a problem for individuals when processing PII—a problematic data action—and the impact of the problematic data action should it occur.

This report concludes with a general roadmap for evolving these preliminary concepts into actionable guidance—complementary to existing NIST guidance for information security risk management—so that agencies may more effectively meet their obligations under Circular A-130 and other relevant policies.

Table of Contents

List of Appendices

List of Figures

1   Introduction

NIST research in information technology—including cybersecurity, cloud computing, big data, and the Smart Grid and other cyber-physical *systems*—aims to improve the innovation and competitiveness that bring great advancements to U.S. national and economic security and quality of life. Much of this research pertains to the *trustworthiness* of these information technologies and the systems in which they are incorporated.

Given concerns about how information technologies may affect privacy at individual and societal levels, building trustworthy systems demands the development of consistent approaches and guidance for translating widely recognized, high-level privacy principles—such as the Fair Information Practice Principles (FIPPs)—into effective *system privacy requirements*.[2]

To date, NIST guidance on the trustworthiness of systems has focused primarily on frameworks and processes that address the security objectives of confidentiality, integrity and availability.[3] Although unauthorized access to *personally identifiable information* (PII) is a subset of information security and a critical aspect of privacy, there is a far less developed understanding of how the system impacts the individuals' privacy and how to identify and address *risks* that extend beyond unauthorized access to PII.[4]

Trustworthiness & Privacy

Trustworthiness simply means worthy of being trusted to fulfill whatever critical requirements may be needed for a particular component, subsystem, system, network, application, mission, enterprise, or other entity.[1]

From a privacy perspective, a trustworthy system is a system that meets specific privacy requirements in addition to meeting other critical requirements.

---

[1] Special Publication 800-160, "Systems Security Engineering: Considerations for a Multidisciplinary Approach in the Engineering of Trustworthy Secure Systems," NIST (NOV 2016) at p. 1, https://doi.org/10.6028/NIST.SP.800-160 [hereinafter known as "NIST SP 800-160"].

[2] In response to privacy concerns arising from the increasing digitization of data, the Code of Fair Information Practice first appeared in a 1973 report by the U.S. Department of Health, Education, and Welfare, "Records Computers and the Rights of Citizens," at p. 41-42, *available at* http://www.justice.gov/opcl/docs/rec-com-rights.pdf). The Code has since evolved into a more comprehensive set of principles known as the Fair Information Practice Principles (FIPPs) that have been adopted in various forms in law and policy within the U.S. government, as well as by international organizations such as the Organization for Economic Cooperation and Development (OECD) and the European Union (see e.g., "Privacy Act of 1974," 5 U.S.C. § 552a, *available at* https://www.gpo.gov/fdsys/pkg/USCODE-2012-title5/pdf/USCODE-2012-title5-partI-chap5-subchapII-sec552a.pdf; "OECD Guidelines for Multinational Enterprises," OECD Publishing *available at* http://www.oecd.org/corporate/mne/1922428.pdf ; "European Parliament and Council Directive 95/46/EC" (1995), *available at* http://ec.europa.eu/justice/policies/privacy/docs/95-46-ce/dir1995-46_part1_en.pdf). Another well-known set of privacy principles related to the FIPPs is Ann Cavoukian's 7 Foundational Principles of Privacy by Design *available at* https://www.iab.org/wp-content/IAB-uploads/2011/03/fred_carter.pdf.

[3] "Federal Information Security Management Act of 2014," 44 U.S.C. § 3552. Definitions, *available at* https://www.gpo.gov/fdsys/pkg/USCODE-2015-title44/pdf/USCODE-2015-title44-chap35-subchapII-sec3552.pdf.

[4] Office of Management and Budget defines PII as "information that can be used to distinguish or trace an individual's identity, either alone or when combined with other information that is linked or linkable to a specific individual," in Circular A-130, "Managing Federal Information as a Strategic Resource" (2016), *available at* https://www.whitehouse.gov/sites/default/files/omb/assets/OMB/circulars/a130/a130revised.pdf [hereinafter known as "Circular A-130"]. It should be noted that this definition is broad and extends beyond commonly understood biographical information to include any information that can be linked to an individual, including behavioral or transactional information.

For example, as part of its work with Smart Grid technology, NIST and its partners in the energy sector have noted public concern regarding the deployment of smart meters due to the ability of these meters to collect, record, and distribute highly granular information about household electrical use. Such information could be used, for example, to learn when a house was occupied and what appliances they were using. A report on this general topic concluded: "While many of the types of data items accessible through the smart grid are not new, there is now the possibility that other parties, entities or individuals will have access to those data items; there are also many new uses for and ways to analyze the collected data, which may raise substantial privacy concerns."[5]

In another example, as part of President Obama's Precision Medicine Initiative (PMI),[6] the Veteran's Administration's Privacy Impact Assessment (PIA) for its Genomic Information System for Integrated Science research program cataloged specific risks, including, but not limited to:

- "The re-identification of information linked to a specific individual, notwithstanding representations that a participant's information would be anonymous or not identifiable…
- Participants misunderstand or underestimate the extent to which they have consented to share their data…
- The perception of a loss of medical or other privacy leading to a change in behavior.
- Embarrassment or stigma associated with certain information should that information be released or tied to the individual…
- Perceived or real risks that information could be used to discriminate against a group of individuals in different *contexts* such as employment or insurance discrimination…
- Information is accessed by law enforcement for reasons beyond research…"[7]

There are many other examples of systems that raise these types of privacy concerns, including ones in urban operations, transportation, and big data analytics.[8] These examples also demonstrate that determining the boundary of a system is an important consideration because privacy concerns can arise at any point where PII is *processed*, including, but not limited to collection, creation, analysis, use, storage, dissemination, disclosure, or disposal. A system boundary is often related to the scope of authorization for operating the system; however, there may be stages of PII processing occurring outside of this authorization scope that give rise to privacy concerns in the system.[9]

---

[5] Interagency Report 7628 Revision 1, "Guidelines for Smart Grid Cybersecurity: Volume II – Privacy and the Smart Grid," NIST (SEPT 2014) at p. 7, https://doi.org/10.6028/NIST.IR.7628r1 [hereinafter known as "NISTIR 7628 Rev1"].

[6] "The Precision Medicine Initiative," The White House, *available at* https://www.whitehouse.gov/precision-medicine.

[7] "Privacy Impact Assessment for the VA Information Technology System called: Million Veteran Program – Genomic Information System for Integrated Science (GENISIS)," Department of Veterans Affairs, Veterans Health Administration, Office of Research and Development (ORD) (JULY 2016), *available at* http://www.oprm.va.gov/docs/PIA/MVP_GENISIS_PIA_20160727.pdf [hereinafter known as "GENESIS"].

[8] See infra Appendix E, "Cyber-Physical Systems" [hereinafter known as "Appendix E"].

[9] Infra section 2.3.1 for further discussion of privacy and system boundaries. NIST Special Publication 800-37 Revision 1 defines security authorization as "the official management decision given by a senior organizational official to authorize operation of an information system and to explicitly accept the risk to organizational operations and assets, individuals, other organizations, and the Nation based on the implementation of an agreed-upon set of security controls." Special Publication 800-37 Revision 1, "Guide for Applying the Risk Management Framework to Federal Information Systems: A Security Life Cycle Approach," NIST (FEB 2010, updated June 5, 2014) at p. 2, footnote 10, https://doi.org/10.6028/NIST.SP.800-37r1

In July 2016, the Office of Management and Budget (OMB) released an update to Circular No. A-130 that requires agencies to apply the NIST Risk Management Framework (RMF) in their privacy programs. That OMB update also includes a new emphasis on managing privacy risk beyond solely compliance with privacy laws, regulations and policies.[10] Although agencies should already be using PIAs to address privacy risk,[11] it is more difficult for them to do it consistently in the absence of a model that enables a repeatable and measurable process to assess privacy risk. Repeatability is important so that the process can be performed consistently over time (not that the outcome is necessarily the same each time). Measurability matters, so that agencies can demonstrate the effectiveness of *privacy controls* in addressing identified privacy risks.

1.1   Purpose and Scope

This publication:

- Lays the groundwork for future guidance on how federal agencies will be able to incorporate privacy as an attribute of trustworthy systems through the management of privacy as a collaborative, interdisciplinary engineering practice;

- Introduces a set of objectives for *privacy engineering* and a new model for assessing privacy risks in federal systems; and

- Provides a roadmap for evolving these preliminary concepts into actionable guidance, complementary to existing NIST guidance for information security risk management, so that agencies may more effectively meet their obligations under Circular A-130 and other relevant policies.[12]

This is an introductory report intended to foster further discussion. Future development of guidance comprehensive enough to promote compliance with policy directives will be conducted

---

[hereinafter known as "NIST SP 800-37 Rev1"].

[10] "Circular A-130," *supra* note 4.

[11] PIAs are generally required under the "E-Government Act of 2002" codified at 44 U.S.C. § 101, *available at* https://www.gpo.gov/fdsys/pkg/PLAW-107publ347/pdf/PLAW-107publ347.pdf. See also, "Circular A-130," *supra* note 4, "A PIA is one of the most valuable tools Federal agencies use to ensure compliance with applicable privacy requirements and manage privacy risks." Id. at Appendix II-10.

[12] See e.g., Office of Management and Budget, Executive Office of the President, "Model Privacy Impact Assessment for Agency Use of Third-Party Websites and Applications" (DEC 2011), *available at* https://www.whitehouse.gov/sites/default/files/omb/inforeg/info_policy/model-pia-agency-use-third-party-websites-and-applications.pdf; Memorandum M-07-16, "Safeguarding Against and Responding to the Breach of Personally Identifiable Information" (MAY 2007), *available at* https://www.whitehouse.gov/sites/default/files/omb/assets/omb/memoranda/fy2007/m07-16.pdf; Memorandum M-10-22, "Guidance for Online Use of Web Measurement and Customization Technologies" (JUNE 2010), *available at* https://www.whitehouse.gov/sites/default/files/omb/assets/memoranda_2010/m10-22.pdf; Memorandum M-10-23, "Guidance for Agency Use of Third-Party Websites and Applications" (JUNE 2010), *available at* https://www.whitehouse.gov/sites/default/files/omb/assets/memoranda_2010/m10-23.pdf; Memorandum M-05-08, "Designation of Senior Agency Officials for Privacy" (FEB 2005), *available at* https://www.whitehouse.gov/sites/default/files/omb/assets/omb/memoranda/fy2005/m05-08.pdf; Memorandum M-03-22, "OMB Guidance for Implementing the Privacy Provisions of the E-Government Act of 2002," *available at* https://www.whitehouse.gov/omb/memoranda_m03-22. See also, National Science and Technology Council: Networking and Information Technology Research and Development Program, "National Privacy Research Strategy" (2016) at p. 9, *available at* https://www.whitehouse.gov/sites/default/files/nprs_nstc_review_final.pdf.

through collaborative and open processes in order to better support the operational needs of agency privacy programs.

1.2 Audience

Addressing privacy is a cross-organizational challenge. To do so effectively, agencies need consistent terminology as well as common processes that complement existing enterprise risk management and *systems engineering* processes. The audience for this document includes those involved in developing systems and evaluating risk, including individuals with:

- Privacy and/or system oversight responsibilities (e.g., senior agency officials for privacy, chief information officers, chief information security officers, agency heads, chief privacy officers);

- Implementation and operational responsibilities in systems, including responsibilities for risk management and the development of security and privacy plans (e.g., mission/business owners, system owners, information owners/stewards, system administrators, system security officers, privacy officers, analysts);

- System engineering and design responsibilities (e.g., program or project managers, system engineers, chief architects); and

- Independent oversight and/or accountability responsibility for privacy (e.g., inspectors general, internal auditors).

1.3 Organization of this Document

The remainder of this report is organized as follows:

- **Chapter 2** explores systems engineering and risk management and their applicability to privacy as distinct from information security,

- **Chapter 3** introduces privacy engineering objectives and a privacy risk model as new conceptual tools needed for conducting privacy engineering and risk management, and

- **Chapter 4** sets forth a roadmap and next steps for the development of comprehensive guidance for federal agencies on privacy engineering and risk management.

This document also includes six appendices:

- **Appendix A** provides background on the NIST research process,

- **Appendix B** is a glossary of terms,

- **Appendix C** explains acronyms,

- **Appendix D** lists references,

- **Appendix E** provides examples of cases where the primary privacy concerns do not arise from security concerns of unauthorized access to PII, and

- **Appendix F** provides the Circular A-130 FIPPs.

2   An Engineering Approach to Privacy

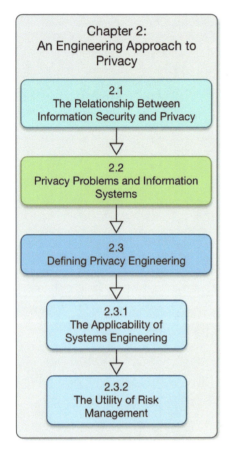

Figure 1: Chapter 2 Flow

Protecting privacy is often said to require a multidisciplinary approach including law, sociology, information security, ethics, and economics.[13] This plurality helps to explain the variety of definitions and terms that describe privacy.[14] Regardless, privacy exists—or is lost—at the boundary line between the individual and others. This boundary is in a state of flux, depending on the context within which a person operates and the degree of value derived from interactions with other people.[15]

Technology exerts pressure on this boundary. Technological improvements can provide tremendous individual and societal benefits, but they also can have adverse effects on privacy at both the individual and societal levels. The ideal system would optimize benefits to the individual and society while minimizing the adverse effects.

This chapter explores how systems engineering and risk management processes could be used to integrate multidisciplinary approaches that can be incorporated into effective privacy solutions.

2.1   The Relationship Between Information Security and Privacy

A significant body of work already addresses security in federal systems.[16] Recently, the term "privacy" has begun to be added to these security documents.[17] This addition implies that privacy shares enough

---

[13] See e.g., "National Privacy Research Strategy," *supra* note 12, and H. Jeff Smith, Tamara Dinev, and Heng Xu, "Information Privacy Research: An Interdisciplinary Review," 35(4) MIS Quarterly at p. 989-1015 (2011), *available at* https://www.researchgate.net/publication/220260183_Information_Privacy_Research_An_Interdisciplinary_Review.

[14] See e.g., Regarding privacy as a human right, Article 12 of the UN "Universal Declaration of Human Rights" states: "No one shall be subjected to arbitrary interference with his privacy, family, home or correspondence, nor to attacks upon his honour and reputation. Everyone has the right to the protection of the law against such interference or attacks." *Available at* http://www.ohchr.org/EN/UDHR/Documents/UDHR_Translations/eng.pdf; viewing privacy tradeoffs with a cost/benefit analysis, see Jule Polonetsky, Omer Tene, and Joseph Jerome, "Benefit-Risk Analysis for Big Data Projects," Future of Privacy Forum (SEPT 2014), *available at* https://fpf.org/wp-content/uploads/FPF_DataBenefitAnalysis_FINAL.pdf; for a review of the legal precedents of privacy, Executive Office of the President, "Big Data: Seizing Opportunities, Preserving Values" (2014), *available at* https://www.whitehouse.gov/sites/default/files/docs/big_data_privacy_report_may_1_2014.pdf.

[15] For a discussion of context, see section 2.3.1 of the "National Privacy Research Strategy," *supra* note 12.

[16] For example, the NIST Computer Security Resource Center provides a broad range of security-related information *available at* http://csrc.nist.gov/.

[17] Special Publication 800-53 Revision 4, "Security and Privacy Controls for Federal Information Systems and Organizations," NIST (APRIL 2013, updated January 22, 2015), *available at* https://doi.org/10.6028/NIST.SP.800-53r4 [hereinafter known as "NIST SP 800-53 Rev4"]; see also Special Publication 800-53A Revision 4, "Assessing Security and Privacy Controls in Federal Information Systems and Organizations," NIST (DEC 2014, updated December 18, 2014), *available at* https://doi.org/10.6028/NIST.SP.800-53Ar4.

characteristics with security that the guidance should be applicable to address privacy. However, using "privacy" as a separate term presumes that privacy has a meaning and brings with it issues distinct from security. That is why it is important to understand the relationship—particularly the distinctions—between information security and privacy. Doing so will improve understanding of how to apply established systems engineering and risk management processes to addressing privacy concerns.

As noted in Circular A-130: "Federal information is a strategic asset subject to risks that must be managed to minimize harm; Protecting an individual's privacy is of utmost importance. The Federal Government shall consider and protect an individual's privacy throughout the information life cycle; While security and privacy are independent and separate disciplines, they are closely related, and it is essential for agencies to take a coordinated approach to identifying and managing security and privacy risks and complying with applicable requirements."[18] At the same time, throughout the Circular, there is a clear recognition that separate leadership with unique skill sets is required for privacy and security and that a coordinated approach does not necessarily mean an identical approach.[19]

Public discourse on the relationship between security and privacy often includes colloquial phrases such as "security and privacy are two sides of a coin" and "there is no privacy without security."[20] In addition, security is typically recognized as one of the FIPPs.[21] There is a clear recognition that confidentiality of PII plays an important role in the protection of privacy.

However, there are security issues unrelated to privacy (e.g., confidentiality of trade secrets), just as there are privacy issues unrelated to security. A number of other FIPPs address the creation, collection, use, processing, retention, dissemination, or disclosure of PII.[22] For example, in the energy sector, some communities have responded negatively to smart meters due largely to concern that the information being collected can reveal behavior inside a person's home, and less so from concerns that the utilities cannot keep the information secure.[23] Even actions taken to

> ### Circular A-130 FIPPs
>
> - **Access and Amendment**
> - **Accountability**
> - **Authority**
> - **Minimization**
> - **Quality and Integrity**
> - **Individual Participation**
> - **Purpose Specification and Use Limitation**
> - **Security**
> - **Transparency**

---

[18] See "Circular A-130," *supra* note 4 at p. 4.

[19] Ibid.

[20] Elain Spear, "Data Privacy and Data Security; Two Sides of the Same Coin A Conversation with Patrick Manzo, Executive Vice President, Global Customer Service and Chief Privacy Officer of Monster Worldwide, Inc," The National Law Review (MAY 2015), *available at* http://www.natlawreview.com/article/data-privacy-and-data-security-two-sides-same-coin-conversation-patrick-manzo-execut; Eija Paajanen, "There is no Privacy Without Security," Business Security News (JULY 2015) *available at* https://business.f-secure.com/there-is-no-privacy-without-security.

[21] See "Circular A-130," *supra* note 4 at Appendix II – Responsibilities for Managing Personally Identifiable Information ("Organizations should protect PII (in all media) through appropriate security safeguards against risks such as loss, unauthorized access or use, destruction, modification, or unintended or inappropriate disclosure").

[22] Ibid. See Appendix F, "The Fair Information Practice Principles (FIPPs)," for full descriptions.

[23] Chris Hooks, "As Towns Say No, Signs of Rising Resistance to Smart Meters," New York Times (MAY 2013), *available at* http://www.nytimes.com/2013/05/26/us/as-texas-towns-say-no-signs-of-rising-resistance-to-smart-meters.html?_r=0; Federico Guerrini, "Smart Meters: Between Economic Benefits and Privacy Concerns," Forbes (JUNE 2014), *available at* http://www.forbes.com/sites/federicoguerrini/2014/06/01/smart-meters-friends-or-foes-between-economic-benefits-and-

protect PII can have privacy implications. For example, security tools, such as persistent activity monitoring, can create concerns about the degree to which information is revealed about individuals that is unrelated to cybersecurity purposes.[24]

These cases illustrate that systems designed to achieve beneficial objectives (e.g., improved efficiency of the electrical grid and increased security) can adversely affect individuals' privacy as an unintended consequence or byproduct of the system as it is *processing* information about individuals.[25]

This byproduct risk model is conceptually distinct from the security risk model. In the security risk model, concerns focus on unauthorized activity that causes a loss of confidentiality, integrity or availability of information or systems. In the byproduct risk model, the processing of PII is planned and permissible (i.e. authorized), but it creates implications for individuals' privacy. So while some privacy concerns arise from unauthorized activity, privacy concerns also can arise from authorized processing of information about individuals.

Figure 2 shows a non-proportional representation of the relationship between the privacy and security domains.

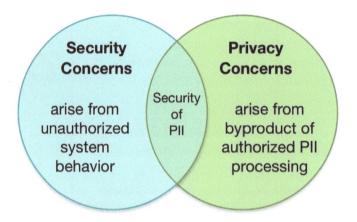

Figure 2: Relationship Between Information Security and Privacy

Recognizing the boundaries and overlap between privacy and security is key to determining when existing security risk models and security-focused guidance may be applied to address privacy concerns—and where there are gaps that need to be filled in order to achieve an engineering approach to privacy. For instance, existing information security guidance does not address the consequences of a poor consent mechanism for use of PII, the purpose of

---

privacy-concerns/; Samuel J. Harvey, "Smart Meters, Smarter Regulation: Balancing Privacy and Innovation in the Electric Grid," 61 UCLA L. Rev. 2068, 2076-90 (2014), *available at* http://www.uclalawreview.org/pdf/61-6-10.pdf. For a discussion regarding privacy risks weighed against big data opportunities, *see* Jules Polonetsky and Omer Tene, "Privacy and Big Data: Making Ends Meet," 66 Stan. L. Rev. 25 (2013), *available at* https://cyberlaw.stanford.edu/files/publication/files/PolonetskyTene.pdf.

[24] "Appendix E," *supra* note 8.

[25] For the purposes of this publication, the use of the term "processing" means the full data life cycle from collection through disposal in accordance with ISO/IEC 29100:2011(E). See "Information technology—Security techniques—Privacy Framework," *available at* http://standards.iso.org/ittf/PubliclyAvailableStandards/c045123_ISO_IEC_29100_2011.zip [hereinafter known as "ISO/IEC 29100:2011(E)"]. Also see Appendix B, "Glossary."

transparency, what PII is being collected, or which changes in use of PII are permitted so long as authorized personnel are conducting the activity. Given these material distinctions in the disciplines, it should be clear that agencies will not be able to effectively manage privacy solely on the basis of managing security.

2.2   Privacy Problems and Systems

As described in section 2.1, privacy concerns in systems arise from authorized processing of PII as well as unauthorized access to PII.[26] The dimension of these concerns can be expressed as a spectrum of problems that people may experience as a result of the information processing. The term "privacy problem" to express an adverse experience resulting from PII processing is not the only term that may be used. Other terms include: privacy harm, privacy violation, privacy intrusion, and privacy invasion.[27] This report uses "privacy problems" with the goal of enabling system engineers and privacy specialists to more dispassionately discuss the potential adverse consequences arising from the manner in which the system is processing PII.[28]

The problems that can result from *unauthorized access* to PII are generally well-recognized. They include embarrassment or other emotional distress from the unauthorized release of information, economic loss from identity theft, or physical or psychological harm from "stalking." Problems from authorized processing may be less visible or not as well understood, but they also result in real consequences. For example, the scope of information collection related to providing public benefits may have a discriminatory and stigmatizing effect on recipients.[29] Inaccurate information or the inability to correct it can lead to frustrations in ordinary activities such as boarding airplanes.[30] Concerns about privacy and systems can cause a loss of trust that results in reluctance to adopt certain products and services that could be beneficial.[31] These concerns could even contribute to systemic failures in our democratic

---

[26] Cyber-physical systems add an extra dimension in so far as they may do more than just process PII. They can also affect people's autonomy over their physical behavior or activities. For example, law enforcement may be able to remotely pull over automated vehicles with passengers inside; see Scott Martelle, "Self-driving cars and the liability issues they raise." Protect Consumer Justice (MAY 2012), *available at* http://www.protectconsumerjustice.org/self-driving-cars-and-the-liability-issues-they-raise.html [hereinafter known as "Self-Driving Cars"]. Smart cities technologies can be used to alter or influence people's behavior such as where or how they move through the city; see Tod Newcombe, "Security, Privacy, Governance Concerns About Smart City Technologies Grow," GovTech (JUNE 2016), *available at* http://www.govtech.com/Security-Privacy-Governance-Concerns-About-Smart-City-Technologies-Grow.html. Further consideration should be given to whether the term PII alone is adequate to cover these concerns.

[27] See Daniel J. Solove, "A Taxonomy of Privacy," U. PA. L. Review, volume 154 at p. 477-484 (2006), *available at* https://www.law.upenn.edu/journals/lawreview/articles/volume154/issue3/Solove154U.Pa.L.Rev.477(2006).pdf. Since the concept of "privacy" is a vague notion, Solove developed a useful privacy taxonomy wherein he focused on the specific activities that pose privacy problems for individuals. See also "National Privacy Research Strategy," *supra* note 12.

[28] Use of the term 'privacy problem' in this publication is for discussion purposes only and is not intended to convey or imply any legal or regulatory conclusion or consequence.

[29] See Khiara M. Bridges, "Privacy Rights and Public Families," 34 Harvard Journal of Law and Gender at p. 113 (2011), *available at* http://www.law.harvard.edu/students/orgs/jlg/vol341/113-174.pdf.

[30] Khaki Ateqah, "No Fly List Grows, Along With Injustice For Those Wrongly Stuck On It" (FEB 2012), *available at* https://www.aclu.org/blog/no-fly-list-grows-along-injustice-those-wrongly-stuck-it.

[31] World Economic Forum, "Rethinking Personal Data: A New Lens for Strengthening Trust" (MAY 2014) at p. 18, *available at* http://www3.weforum.org/docs/WEF_RethinkingPersonalData_ANewLens_Report_2014.pdf [hereinafter known as "Rethinking Personal Data"].

institutions, such as voting.[32] The consequences of these experiences can impact quality of life at both a personal and societal level. It is vital, therefore, that engineers understand the issue and have the conceptual tools to build systems that minimize problems for individuals when processing their information.

Figure 3 illustrates a range of problems that can arise from processing PII.[33]

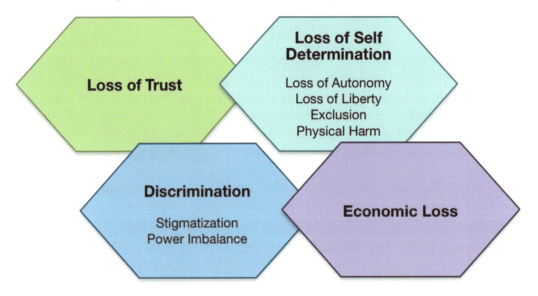

Figure 3: Potential Problems Arising from the Processing of PII

Figure 3 is for illustrative purposes only. It does not purport to capture the full scope of problems people could experience from the processing of their information, nor is it the only way to describe these problems. However, if agencies are to bridge the distance between privacy principles and their effective implementation in systems, they will need transformative concepts that align with existing engineering and risk management processes. The objective for introducing the terminology in Figure 3 is to initiate a broader discussion of privacy problems as the basis for identifying outcomes for privacy that can be achieved through the use of engineering and risk management processes. The results of such a broader discussion may include the refinement of this terminology to ease use in cross-organizational assessments.

2.3 Defining Privacy Engineering

There is no widely-accepted definition of the term "privacy engineering." For purposes of this publication, privacy engineering means a specialty discipline of systems engineering focused on

---

[32] See Ira S. Rubinstein, "Voter privacy in the age of big data," Wisconsin Law Review (2014) at p. 905-6, *available at* http://wisconsinlawreview.org/wp-content/uploads/2015/02/1-Rubinstein-Final-Online.pdf. Rubenstein discusses how large scale data analytics can create privacy concerns in the electoral process outside of the ballot box: "Indeed, there is a very strong argument that campaign data practices and voter microtargeting undermine anonymous speech by subjecting voters to a form of political surveillance in which their beliefs and preferences are monitored and tracked.... the freedom to read anonymously suggests that voters are entitled to seek and gain access to online political information without having to disclose their political leanings or suffer the chilling effect of pervasive monitoring and tracking of their every thought and belief."

[33] The content of Figure 3 is derived from Daniel Solove's, "A Taxonomy of Privacy," *supra* note 27.

achieving freedom from conditions that can create problems for individuals with unacceptable consequences that arise from the system as it processes PII.[34] This definition provides an independent frame of reference that has been lacking in the privacy field. Many agencies use the FIPPs as longstanding foundational principles for the fair handling of PII. The FIPPs have enduring value by articulating expectations regarding appropriate information practices, and they have helped many organizations to develop baseline considerations for protecting individuals' privacy as new technologies enter the marketplace. As some have noted though:

"They [the FIPPs] are value statements rather than recipes, however. System planners often encounter difficulties when trying to operationalize them, particularly when assessing privacy risks and when establishing privacy requirements for designing and developing systems and technologies. Those activities require a well-articulated set of privacy objectives and a privacy risk assessment approach, from which privacy risks can be evaluated and implementation requirements can be developed."[35]

Or put another way, evaluating how the FIPPs should be applied, particularly across different types of systems, without an independent frame of reference, provides no point of comparison.[36] Experienced privacy officers may have a knowledge base about privacy concerns that enables them to sufficiently analyze the FIPPs. However, this type of ad hoc analysis contributes little to the development of a repeatable and measurable process that can be understood and communicated inside and outside the organization.

In contrast, being explicit about a desired, identifiable outcome—systems that minimize the creation

---

Privacy and System Boundaries

In addition to its importance in the context of the NIST Risk Management Framework, the boundary of a system is an important consideration for privacy engineering. In the Glossary of NIST SP 800-160, the term "system-of-interest" is used to describe the system that is the focus of the systems engineering effort, and notes that the boundary of the system-of-interest is typically determined relative to the authorization boundary. However, it can also be determined by other "boundaries" established by programmatic, operational, or jurisdictional control.[37]

Although it is the responsibility of an agency to determine the boundaries of a system, as noted, privacy risks can arise at any stage of PII *processing* from collection through disposal. In some circumstances, system owners may consider these stages to take place outside the typical authorization boundary. Thus, agencies may instead need to take a programmatically expansive view of the boundary of a system in order to fully assess privacy risk.

---

[34] See "Appendix E," *supra* note 8 for considerations about the comprehensiveness of the term "PII" and the implications for privacy engineering in cyber-physical systems. In addition, for a related discussion about the definition of systems security engineering see "NIST SP 800-160," *supra* note 1.

[35] Stuart S. Shapiro, et al., "MITRE Response to OSTP/NITRD 'National Privacy Research Strategy' RFI," MITRE Corporation (AUG 2014) at p. 8, *available at* https://www.nitrd.gov/cybersecurity/nprsrfi102014/MITRE.pdf.

[36] "First, they [the FIPPs] are relative with respect to purpose, permitting PII collection and use for essentially any reason, no matter how fundamentally inimical to privacy. Second, they encourage framing of privacy harms purely in terms of principle violations, as opposed to the actual impact on individuals." Stuart S. Shapiro, "Situating Anonymization Within a Privacy Risk Model," Homeland Security Systems Engineering and Development Institute (2012) at p. 2, *available at* https://www.mitre.org/sites/default/files/pdf/12_0353.pdf.

[37] "NIST SP 800-160," *supra* note 1.

of problems arising from the processing of PII—provides a clear and common purpose that can be understood at all organizational levels of an agency.

Moreover, this outcome-based focus provides the frame of reference that can facilitate translation of privacy principles into system privacy requirements. For instance, a system requirement could be "to limit the collection of a particular set of data that may create problems for individuals—without impeding the functionality of the system" rather than an abstract statement about minimizing the data to be collected. Privacy officers would still be called upon to apply their expertise in identifying the nature of the problem, but system engineers, by gaining an understanding of a clear privacy outcome, would be better positioned to become collaborative partners in the process of building more trustworthy systems. Section 2.3.1 offers additional considerations about why systems engineering and privacy are compatible disciplines.

The other notable part of the privacy engineering definition offered in this report is its recognition of risk acceptance inherent in the clause "problems for individuals with unacceptable consequences." Just as there is no system that can be perfectly free of security risk, there can be no expectation that all privacy risk can be eliminated from a system when it is processing PII. Section 2.3.2 introduces risk management as a key systems engineering process to support agencies in how to make determinations about what constitutes unacceptable consequences.

2.3.1 The Applicability of Systems Engineering

An important objective of systems engineering is to deliver systems deemed trustworthy.[38] As described in NIST SP 800-160:

> "Systems engineering is a collection of system life cycle technical and nontechnical processes with associated activities and tasks. The technical processes apply engineering analysis and design principles to deliver a system with the capability to satisfy stakeholder requirements and critical quality properties. The nontechnical processes provide for engineering management of all aspects of the engineering project, agreements between parties involved in the engineering project, and project-enabling support to facilitate execution of the engineering project. Systems engineering efforts are a very complex undertaking that requires the close coordination between the engineering team and stakeholders throughout the various stages of the system life cycle."[39]

This description of systems engineering as a holistic process that must account for the needs and expectations of stakeholders is particularly relevant for privacy.[40] Individuals as stakeholders may not have a tangible role in the system design process. However, utilizing processes of systems engineering could enable system engineers to take individuals' privacy interests into

---

[38] "NIST SP 800-160," *supra* note 1 at p. 8.
[39] Ibid.
[40] ISO/IEC/IEEE 15288, ("Systems and software engineering – System life cycle processes" (MAY 2015), *available at* http://www.iso.org/iso/catalogue_detail?csnumber=63711 [hereinafter known as "ISO/IEC/IEEE 15288"]) covers 30 processes that span an organization including acquisition, human resources management, business or mission analysis, risk management, and operation.

account, resulting in a system that may be less likely to create problems for them.

Based on the precepts of systems engineering, privacy engineering could help to ensure that the appropriate privacy principles are applied across an agency and throughout the system life cycle to achieve stakeholder objectives for protecting individual privacy. Privacy engineering also can provide a sufficient base of evidence to support claims that the desired level of trustworthiness has been achieved. It can leverage the holistic processes of systems engineering to integrate other engineering specialties such as software engineering, as well as other multi-disciplinary approaches to privacy, including research in fields such as usability and socio-economics.

This section introduced systems engineering's potential to enable privacy to be included as a key attribute of trustworthy systems. It also provides a foundation for the discussion in chapter 3 about new conceptual tools that could better support engineers in this effort. Nonetheless, more research is needed to explore the potential benefits and limitations of applying systems engineering to privacy and to refine the definition of privacy engineering as necessary.[41]

2.3.2 The Utility of Risk Management

Systems engineering balances the often conflicting design constraints of performance, cost, schedule, and effectiveness to optimize the solution while providing an acceptable level of risk.[42] Risk management is a key process that enables agencies to achieve mission goals while minimizing adverse outcomes. By providing a common language to address risks, risk management is especially helpful in communicating inside the organization (e.g. across management levels and operating units), as well as outside the organization. Developing a common language and model for privacy risk management that is complementary to other disciplines could help agencies to address privacy risk in greater parity with other risk categories within their broader enterprise risk management portfolio.[43]

NIST has developed guidance for information security risk management—including the RMF, and guidance on risk assessment—which has informed much of the approach introduced in this report.[44] Although the concept of privacy risk is not new to federal policy, to date there has been no guidance on how to assess this risk.[45] Outside the federal government, standards such as the International Organization for Standardization (ISO) Privacy Framework and the Organization for the Advancement of Structured Information Standards (OASIS) Privacy Management Reference Model include provisions for privacy risk assessment as part of their frameworks or methodologies, but they do not provide guidance on how to actually conduct a risk assessment

---

[41] See the "National Privacy Research Strategy" for a discussion of additional research areas, *supra* note 12 at p. 12.

[42] "NIST SP 800-160," *supra* note 1 at p. 8.

[43] OMB, Circular A-123, "Management's Responsibility for Enterprise Risk Management and Internal Control" (JULY 2016), *available at* https://www.whitehouse.gov/sites/default/files/omb/memoranda/2016/m-16-17.pdf.

[44] Special Publication 800-30 Revision 1, "Guide for Conducting Risk Assessments," NIST (SEPT 2012), https://doi.org/10.6028/NIST.SP.800-30r1 [hereinafter known as "NIST SP 800-30 Rev1"]; see also "NIST SP 800-37 Rev1," *supra* note 9.

[45] There are numerous federal policies that require agencies to address privacy risk, *supra* note 12.

either.[46]

The dearth of risk assessment guidance may be because, until recently, the privacy field has followed a fairly fixed approach to privacy protections due to privacy laws and regulatory policies that have prescribed precise obligations to which an organization must adhere (e.g., providing notices and obtaining consent).[47] Assessments therefore, tend to be focused on compliance rather than the effectiveness of achieving a positive outcome for privacy. For example, assessments are conducted to determine whether a notice regarding privacy exists rather than to evaluate whether people are likely to read that notice and receive some privacy-protective benefit. In contrast, information security laws and regulations may specifically require risk analysis or provide more flexibility in how requirements can be implemented towards a more outcome-based goal of appropriate security.[48]

There is a growing emphasis on risk management for privacy that extends beyond compliance.[49] Organizations including The MITRE Corporation, the Centre for Information Policy Leadership, the iMinds-DistriNet research group at the University of Leuven, and others have published work highlighting the importance of understanding privacy risk in order to improve privacy engineering.[50] Some have specifically cited a need for a risk model for privacy.[51] Section 3.2 explores why the existing information security risk model presents challenges for assessing privacy risks arising from the authorized processing of PII. It also introduces a complementary, but distinct, risk model for privacy.[52]

---

[46] "ISO/IEC 29100:2011(E)," *supra* note 25. Also see "Privacy Management Reference Model and Methodology (PMRM) Version 1.0," OASIS Committee Specification 02 (2016), *available at* http://docs.oasis-open.org/pmrm/PMRM/v1.0/cs02/PMRM-v1.0-cs02.html.

[47] See e.g., "Children's Online Privacy Protection Act," 15 U.S.C. §§ 6501–6506 (1998), *available at* https://www.law.cornell.edu/uscode/text/15/chapter-91; see also "Privacy Act of 1974," *supra* note 2.

[48] "Federal Information Security Management Act of 2014," *supra* note 3.

[49] "Circular A-130," *supra* note 4; see also "European Union General Data Protection Regulation," Regulation (EU) 2016/679 of the European Parliament and of the Council (2016) *available at* http://eur-lex.europa.eu/legal-content/EN/TXT/?uri=CELEX%3A32016R0679.

[50] Stuart S. Shapiro, et al., "Privacy Engineering Framework," The MITRE Corporation (AUG 2014), *available at* http://www.mitre.org/publications/technical-papers/privacy-engineering-framework; Centre for Information Policy Leadership, "Protecting Privacy in a World of Big Data: The Role of Risk Management," Hunton & Williams LLP (FEB 2016), *available at* https://www.informationpolicycentre.com/uploads/5/7/1/0/57104281/protecting_privacy_in_a_world_of_big_data_paper_2_the_role_of_risk_management_16_february_2016.pdf; Centre for Information Policy Leadership, "Risk, High Risk, Risk Assessments and Data Protection Impact Assessments under the GDPR," Hunton & Wiliams LLP (DEC 2016), *available at* https://www.informationpolicycentre.com/uploads/5/7/1/0/57104281/cipl_gdpr_project_risk_white_paper_21_december_2016.pdf; and "LINDDUN: A Privacy Threat Assessment Framework," *available at* https://people.cs.kuleuven.be/~kim.wuyts/LINDDUN/LINDDUN.pdf. In addition, the "NIST Roadmap for Improving Critical Infrastructure Cybersecurity" (FEB 2014) highlights the need for a risk management model, *available at* https://www.nist.gov/sites/default/files/documents/cyberframework/roadmap-021214.pdf.

[51] "Situating Anonymization Within a Privacy Risk Model," *supra* note 36.

[52] Notably, the World Economic Forum has highlighted how security risk models are inappropriate for understanding the full nature of privacy risk. See "Rethinking Personal Data," *supra* note 31, at p. 18.

3   Components for Privacy Engineering in Federal Systems

As noted in the Introduction, agencies should be using PIAs as one of their main tools to address privacy risk. According to Circular A-130, "A PIA is an analysis of how PII is handled to ensure that handling conforms to applicable privacy requirements, determine the privacy risks associated with a system or activity, and evaluate ways to mitigate privacy risks. A PIA is both an analysis and a formal document detailing the process and the outcome of the analysis."[53] However, as discussed in chapter 2, there is a need for more guidance on privacy engineering processes, including the assessment of privacy risk.

Figure 4 illustrates some components of privacy engineering and the results from their use or application in a privacy engineering process. This figure demonstrates how existing components such as the use of laws, regulations and the FIPPs to derive privacy requirements and use of the PIA to describe the system assessment process and results are supplemented by components typically used in information security: a risk model to produce a risk assessment; system objectives (e.g., confidentiality, integrity, availability) to map and evaluate system capabilities in order to provide assurance that the system meets the requirements and addresses risk appropriately; and use of a risk management framework to provide a process for selecting and assessing controls to manage identified risks and meet the requirements.

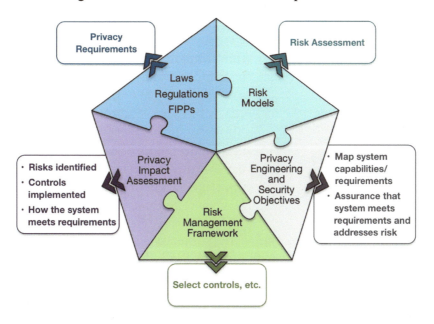

Figure 4: Components of Privacy Engineering

The remainder of this chapter explores how the components of system objectives and a risk model could be defined for privacy.

---

[53] "Circular A-130," *supra* note 4 at Appendix II-10.

3.1   Introducing Privacy Engineering Objectives

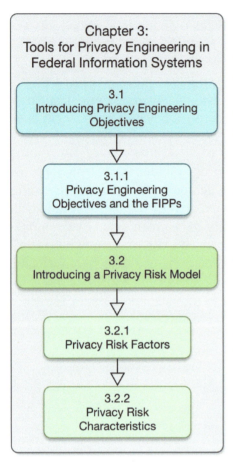

Figure 5: Chapter 3 Flow

Following its public workshop on privacy engineering in April 2014, NIST first focused its efforts on the communication gap between policy and legal teams and the engineering and information technology (IT) teams cited by multiple attendees as being at the core of many of their organizations' privacy challenges.[54] Organizations need systems to support their privacy policies, but the translation from a general set of principles to specific system privacy requirements is not effortless. As discussed in chapter 2, privacy engineering can provide an outcome-oriented process to support this goal.

Privacy engineering also should provide a sufficient base of evidence to supports claims that the desired level of trustworthiness has been achieved. System engineers could use an organizing construct to help them characterize system properties associated with privacy and to map system capabilities and controls to provide evidence of the desired level of trustworthiness.

In information security, the security objectives also known as the CIA triad—confidentiality, integrity, and availability—have been used as a means of categorizing capabilities and controls to achieve security outcomes. Similarly, privacy engineering objectives could enable system designers or engineers to focus on the types of capabilities the system needs in order to demonstrate implementation of an agency's privacy policies and system privacy requirements.

Figure 6 presents three privacy engineering objectives for this purpose. These are not intended to be new statements of policy. As with the CIA triad, these objectives are core characteristics of systems. A system should exhibit each objective in some degree to be considered a system that can support an agency's privacy policies. The privacy engineering objectives are intended to provide a degree of precision to encourage the implementation of measurable controls for managing privacy risk. System designers and engineers, working with policy teams, can use the objectives to help bridge the gap between high-level privacy principles and their implementation within systems.[55]

---

[54] See infra Appendix A for more background. See also the webcast of the "April 2014 NIST Privacy Engineering Workshop," *available at* https://www.nist.gov/computer-security-division/privacy-engineering-workshop-webcast [hereinafter known as "NIST Privacy Engineering Workshop"].

[55] Further research is needed to explore measuring the effectiveness of privacy controls. See e.g., "National Privacy Research Strategy," *supra* note 12, at section 3.3.

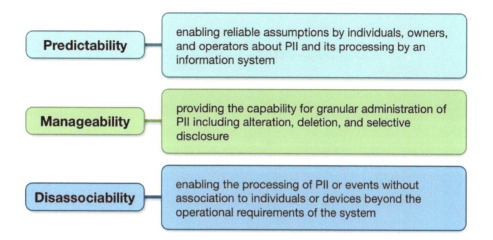

Figure 6: Privacy Engineering Objectives

Figure 7 shows an implementation of the privacy engineering objectives and how they can be used to express capabilities in support of policies.[56] For example, to the extent an agency might have a privacy policy that claims that an identity broker does not have access to user attributes, the technical measures used to implement the capability in the first bullet under *predictability* could be used as a basis for evidence that the agency's privacy policy is a true statement.

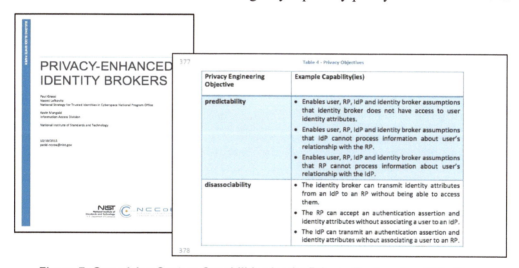

Figure 7: Organizing System Capabilities by the Privacy Engineering Objectives

3.1.1 Privacy Engineering Objectives and the FIPPs

The privacy engineering objectives are intended to supplement, not replace the FIPPs.[57] Figure Figure 8 shows the primary alignments between the Circular A-130 FIPPs and these objectives (as well as the security objectives).

---

[56] Paul Grassi, Naomi Lefkovitz, and Kevin Mangold, "Privacy-Enhanced Identity Brokers," National Institute of Standards and Technology (OCT 2015), *available at* https://nccoe.nist.gov/sites/default/files/library/project-descriptions/privacy-enhanced-identity-brokers-project-description-draft.pdf.

[57] Notably, the information security field also uses principles in addition to objectives. Both have a role in the overall process of systems security engineering. See e.g., "NIST SP 800-160," *supra* note 1 at Appendix F.

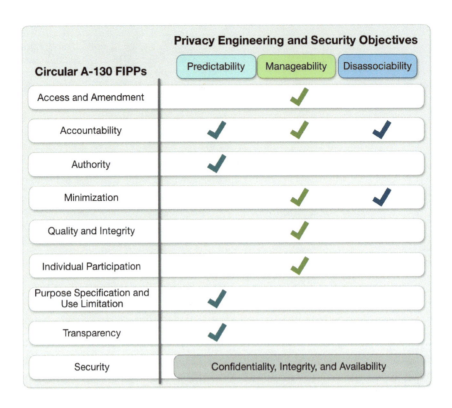

Figure 8: Aligning the Circular A-130 FIPPs to the Privacy Engineering and Security Objectives

3.1.1.1 Predictability

A reliable sense of what is occurring with PII in a system is core to building trust and accountability, and is a primary part of the underlying rationale for the transparency and accountability FIPPs. By framing predictability in terms of reliable assumptions, agencies can begin to measure more concretely the capabilities in a system that supports these principles. For example, if agencies provide notices to inform users about how their information is being handled, an assessment of a notice as a means of enabling reliable assumptions might focus on whether users have read and understood the notice, or even whether they responded as anticipated. Such an assessment could provide significantly more value in determining the efficacy of the privacy control than merely checking whether the notice was provided. Likewise, if system owners and operators can reliably describe what is occurring with PII, they can better maintain accountability for system compliance with organizational privacy policies and system privacy requirements.

Enabling reliable assumptions does not require that each stakeholder knows all the technical details about how a system processes PII.[58] Rather, predictability is about designing systems so that stakeholders are not surprised by the handling of PII.[59] In this

---

[58] Certainly, the IT personnel would be expected to have a complete understanding of how the system operates.

[59] See e.g., Pat Conroy et al., "Building Consumer Trust: Protecting consumer data in the consumer product industry" (NOV 2014), *available at* http://dupress.com/articles/consumer-data-privacy-strategies/, wherein Deloitte reported the results of its recent study of online consumers that showed 80% are "more likely to purchase brands from consumer product companies that they believe protect their personal information."

way, predictability can support a range of organizational interpretations of transparency—from a value statement about the importance of open processes to a requirements-based program that provides for the publication of how PII is managed.

In addition, the predictability objective could promote consideration of a broader range of privacy controls than just notices. For example, use of technical measures such as de-identification techniques could provide evidence that the system's actual disclosures of information align with the assumptions individuals have about what information is being revealed about them.

Predictability also supports the purpose specification and use limitation FIPP without being a constraint on innovation or changes in use of PII. An underlying rationale for this FIPP is the management of the privacy risk associated with changes in context around the use of PII.[60] By focusing on maintaining reliable assumptions about processing of PII, predictability could encourage system operators to assess and address the impact of any changes in that processing.[61] Thus, predictability facilitates the maintenance of stable, trusted relationships between systems and individuals, while enabling operators to continue to innovate and provide better services.

3.1.1.2 Manageability

Manageability is an important system property enabling several of the FIPPs: access and amendment; accountability; minimization; quality and integrity; and individual participation. If agencies cannot administer individuals' information with sufficient granularity, they cannot be confident that inaccurate information can be identified and corrected, obsolete information is disposed of, only necessary information is collected or disclosed, and that individuals' privacy preferences about uses of their information are implemented and maintained.

Nonetheless, manageability is not a policy statement about whether individuals should have the right to control their information, although it could enable a system capability to implement that policy. In certain systems, however, it might impair the mission objective if individuals were able to edit or delete information themselves (e.g., systems for fraud detection or proof of eligibility). Manageability in these systems would still enable the appropriately privileged actor to administer changes to maintain accuracy and fair treatment of individuals. Finally, manageability could support the mapping of technical measures such as data tagging and emerging standards in identity management relating to

---

[60] For a discussion of context see "National Privacy Research Strategy," *supra* note 12. See also "Consumer Data Privacy in a Networked World: A Framework for Protecting Privacy and Promoting Innovation in the Global Digital Economy," The White House (FEB 2012), https://www.whitehouse.gov/sites/default/files/privacy-final.pdf. Following the release of the 2012 Consumer Data Privacy document, the Administration developed and released a discussion draft of a legislative proposal to translate the principles into legislation. "Administration Discussion Draft: Consumer Privacy Bill of Rights Act," The White House (FEB 2015), https://www.whitehouse.gov/sites/default/files/omb/legislative/letters/cpbr-act-of-2015-discussion-draft.pdf.

[61] As discussed in chapter 2, a key objective of privacy engineering is to support organizational processes for managing the risk of adverse outcomes while maintaining mission effectiveness. Policy decisions about changes in PII processing should be made in the larger context of enterprise risk management.

attribute transmission.[62]

3.1.1.3 Disassociability

Disassociability captures one of the elements of privacy-preserving systems—that the system actively protects or "blinds" an individual's identity or associated activities from exposure. Unlike confidentiality, which is focused on preventing unauthorized access to information, disassociability recognizes that privacy risks can result from exposures even within an authorized perimeter. Disassociability advances the capabilities of a privacy-preserving system by engaging system designers and engineers in a deliberate consideration of points of exposure that are not essential for the operation of the system. In this way, it is most closely associated with capabilities that could be used to implement the minimization FIPP.

Although operational requirements may vary depending on the system, achieving this objective should reflect the ability of the system to complete the transaction without associating information with individuals. For example, identity proofing or providing direct health care services may necessitate associating information with an individual. However, an association should not be deemed an operational requirement just because it would be difficult to disassociate the information from individuals. Agencies may opt to knowingly accept the risk, or select controls that require an acceptance of greater residual risk because of the difficulty or cost in implementing stronger controls. The recognition of such risk is distinct from determining that certain information must be associated with an individual to meet an operational requirement.

Many cryptographic techniques that exist today or are currently being researched could be mapped to disassociability.[63] Adopting disassociability as an objective could raise awareness of the benefits of these techniques and increase demand for more advances. A further consideration is whether a taxonomy could be constructed of existing identity-related classifications, including anonymity, de-identification, unlinkability, unobservability, pseudonymity or others.[64] Such a taxonomy could potentially support more precise control mapping and risk mitigation.

3.2   Introducing a Privacy Risk Model

As described in chapter 2, there is an increased emphasis on privacy risk management, but little guidance on how to conduct it. This section describes common risk terminology from NIST guidance and adapts this terminology to provide a new privacy risk model as a first step towards developing guidance for privacy risk assessment.

---

[62] See e.g., Paul A. Grassi, Ellen M. Nadeau, Ryan J. Galluzzo, Abhiraj T. Dinh, NIST Internal Report 8112 (Draft), "Attribute Metadata" (AUG 2016), *available at* http://csrc.nist.gov/publications/drafts/nistir-8112/nistir_8112_draft.pdf.

[63] For instance, the use of the "zero-knowledge proof" cryptographic method could allow one party (the prover) to authenticate an identity to another party (the verifier) without the exchange of private or secret information. Giani, Annarita "Identification with Zero Knowledge Protocols," SANS Institute (2001), *available at* https://www.sans.org/reading-room/whitepapers/vpns/identification-zero-knowledge-protocols-719.

[64] Some of these concepts are explored in NISTIR 8053, "De-Identification of Personal Information" (OCT 2015), https://doi.org/10.6028/NIST.IR.8053. See also "LINDDUN: A Privacy Threat Assessment Framework," which outlines a method for modeling privacy-specific threats, *supra* note 50, and Special Publication 800-188, "De-Identifying Government Datasets," NIST (DEC 2016), *available at* http://csrc.nist.gov/publications/drafts/800-188/sp800_188_draft2.pdf.

Some key risk concepts are:

- Risk is a measure of the extent to which an entity is threatened by a potential circumstance or event, and is typically a function of: (i) the adverse impacts that would arise if the circumstance or event occurs; and (ii) the likelihood of occurrence;

- The process by which risks are identified is called a risk assessment; and

- Risk assessments require a risk model to define the risk factors to be assessed and the relationships among those factors.[65]

In information security, the risk factors include the threats to the system and the vulnerabilities that can be exploited by those threats.[66] However, the terms "threat" and "vulnerability" fail to capture the essence of many privacy problems for individuals. Returning to the example of the smart meters, the smart meters are the part of the system collecting the information and thereby creating the problems for individuals (e.g., loss of trust; chilling effect on ordinary behavior). An information security risk model would be unlikely to perceive this behavior of the smart meter as a "threat" since the activity is an authorized part of the functioning of the system itself. While it is not inconceivable to expand a threat-based model to apply to the purposeful processing of PII, overloading this term runs the risk of causing more confusion and miscommunication than clarity, and ultimately creating more difficulties in determining meaningful privacy risk assessments and appropriate mitigations.

Consequently, agencies need terminology more suited to the nature of privacy in systems to be able to identify privacy risk as distinct from information security risk. As described in section 2.2, the potential circumstance or event of concern is a problem that individuals experience as a byproduct of authorized processing of PII. Therefore, rather than adding more concepts to the term "threat," a more information-rich factor for a privacy risk model is to identify the operation that a system is performing on PII, that could cause an adverse effect or a problem for individuals—in short, a *problematic data action*.

> **Problematic data action** means a *data action* that causes an adverse effect, or problem, for individuals.

3.2.1 Privacy Risk Factors

In the information security risk model the primary risk factors are expressed as the likelihood that a vulnerability will be exploited by a threat and the impact of such occurrence.[67] In the privacy risk model, the problematic data action plays the same functional role in framing the adverse event as do threats in the information security risk model. Agencies could use the privacy risk model to factor the extent to which systems and processes are vulnerable to

---

[65] "NIST SP 800-30 Rev1," *supra* note 44 at p. 6-8.
[66] Id. at p. 8.
[67] Id. at p. 10-11.

problematic data actions as well as the likelihood of a problematic data action, and the impact of the problematic data action should it occur. Just as agencies conduct risk assessments to determine the information security risk of their systems and processes, they will need to conduct risk assessments to determine the privacy risk of their systems and processes by assessing the data actions of their systems, how they may become problematic, as well as what processes or controls they already have in place to manage these concerns. When agencies can assess these factors, they will be able to better assess the likelihood and impact of a problematic data action.

Likelihood in a privacy risk model is the probability that a data action will become problematic for a representative or typical individual whose PII is processed by the system. Users' perceptions of a data action and context are critical to determining likelihood. Agencies can support the assessment of likelihood in a number of ways, including: using existing information on customer demographics, extrapolating from information available about privacy problems in similar scenarios, and conducting focus groups or surveys to learn more about users' privacy interests and concerns to determine whether users may consider a data action to be problematic.

Impact is the magnitude of cost or harm from the problematic data action. The fact that only individuals—not agencies—can directly experience a privacy problem is especially challenging for assessing impact. An effective privacy risk model must capture the potential cost of problems to individuals, but it may be difficult to do with any consistency because there may be a significant divergence in the way individuals experience problems; that holds true especially for embarrassment or other psychologically-based problems. Assessing the impact on individuals is an area that needs further research. However, agencies may be able to use various other costs as proxies to help account for individual impact. They include, but are not limited to:

- legal compliance costs arising from the problems created for individuals,

- mission failure costs such as reluctance to use the system or service,

- reputational costs leading to loss of trust, and

- internal culture costs which impact morale or mission productivity as employees assess their general mission to serve the public good against the problems individuals may experience.

Agencies also can consider expanding repercussions for the federal government, economic and national security, and societal impacts on democratic institutions and quality of life.[68]

In a world of limited resources, an important function of a risk assessment is to prioritize risks to enable determinations about the appropriate response. Risk can be managed, but it cannot be eliminated. Just as security risk management practices are not expected to result in perfect security, privacy risk management should not be seen as a vehicle for creating perfect privacy-preserving systems. To achieve an acceptable degree of residual risk and avoid unacceptable consequences, agencies must be able to reflect their best understanding of the problems individuals may experience through the lens of the benefits derived from mission objectives,

---

[68] "Circular A-130," *supra* note 4 at Appendix II, p. 2.

system performance, security, reliability, safety, resource limitations, etc. A thorough privacy risk assessment should provide a mechanism for agencies to determine an optimal solution that accounts for these needs and constraints.

3.2.2 Privacy Risk Characteristics

Risk factors may be further deconstructed into more detailed characteristics.[69] Chapter 4 lays out a roadmap for developing more detailed guidance on privacy risk characteristics and their role in a risk assessment process. This subsection provides a brief introduction to three key characteristics that could facilitate determination of the likelihood and impact of problematic data actions.

3.2.2.1 Data Actions

Data actions are any system operations that process PII. Processing can include, but is not limited to, the collection, retention, logging, analysis, generation, transformation or merging, disclosure, transfer, and disposal of PII. As detailed above, the privacy risk model hinges on whether a data action becomes problematic for individuals. Thus, a privacy risk assessment should be oriented around the identification of a system's discrete data actions, and subsequent determination of which of these data actions could be problematic.

3.2.2.2 PII

OMB defines PII as information that can be used to distinguish or trace an individual's identity, either alone or when combined with other information that is linked or linkable to a specific individual.[70] Circular A-130 notes that the definition is necessarily broad.[71] Nonetheless, as previously noted in this report, more consideration needs to be given to the effect of cyber-physical systems on human behavior in the physical realm, and how it should be accounted for in a privacy risk model.[72]

3.2.2.3 Context

Context—the circumstances surrounding the system's processing of PII—is the foundation for the interpretative analysis necessary to understanding when a privacy boundary line has been crossed.[73] For instance, an email address used in an office directory may not be problematic in many cases, but an email address linked to an individual with a health condition and disclosed outside of the health care context may lead to problems such as embarrassment or discrimination. Context, therefore, is a key characteristic in determining the likelihood of a data action becoming problematic.

---

[69] "NIST SP 800-30 Rev1," *supra* note 44 at p. 8.
[70] "Circular A-130," *supra* note 4 at p. 33.
[71] Ibid.
[72] *Supra* note 26. See also "Appendix E," *supra* note 8.
[73] Helen Nissenbaum, "Privacy in Context: Technology, Policy, and the Integrity of Social Life," Stanford University Press (NOV 2009).

4   Roadmap for Federal Guidance for Privacy Engineering and Risk Management

The update to OMB Circular A-130 significantly expands the obligations of federal agencies with respect to managing privacy risk around information resources, including the responsibilities of the *Senior Agency Official for Privacy*, application of the NIST RMF, and managing privacy risk beyond compliance with laws, regulations, and policies.[74] The purpose of this publication is to provide an introduction to how systems engineering and risk management could be used to develop more trustworthy systems that include privacy as an integral attribute. However, an introduction is insufficient to provide the detailed guidance federal agencies will need to incorporate these processes into their privacy programs and to meet their responsibilities under OMB Circular A-130.[75]

NIST already has developed extensive guidance for federal agencies on information security risk management, including the establishment of the RMF.[76] With respect to privacy programs, this guidance is appropriate for addressing risks to individuals arising from unauthorized access to their information. As this report notes, however, such guidance is not as well-suited for addressing risk that may arise from the authorized processing of PII. Collaborating through open processes, NIST intends to expand its guidance to enable agencies to apply the privacy risk model and the privacy engineering objectives to existing engineering and risk management practices. The goal of this expanded guidance is to enable greater consistency in achieving privacy-positive outcomes for their systems.[77] In addition, this expanded guidance will help agencies to better integrate the NIST RMF into agencies' privacy programs.

The following figure shows the principal security risk management-related special publications for which NIST plans to develop complementary guidance relevant to privacy:

---

[74] "Circular A-130," *supra* note 4. See also OMB M-16-24 "Role and Designation of Senior Agency Officials for Privacy" (2016) *available at* https://www.whitehouse.gov/sites/default/files/omb/memoranda/2016/m_16_24_0.pdf.

[75] See "Circular A-130," *supra* note 4.

[76] "NIST SP 800-37 Rev1," *supra* note 9; see also Special Publication 800-39 Revision 1, "Managing Information Security Risk," NIST (MARCH 2011), *available at* http://nvlpubs.nist.gov/nistpubs/SpecialPublications/NIST.SP.800-37r1.pdf; and "NIST SP 800-30 Rev1," *supra* note 44.

[77] See "Circular A-130," *supra* note 4 at footnote 121.

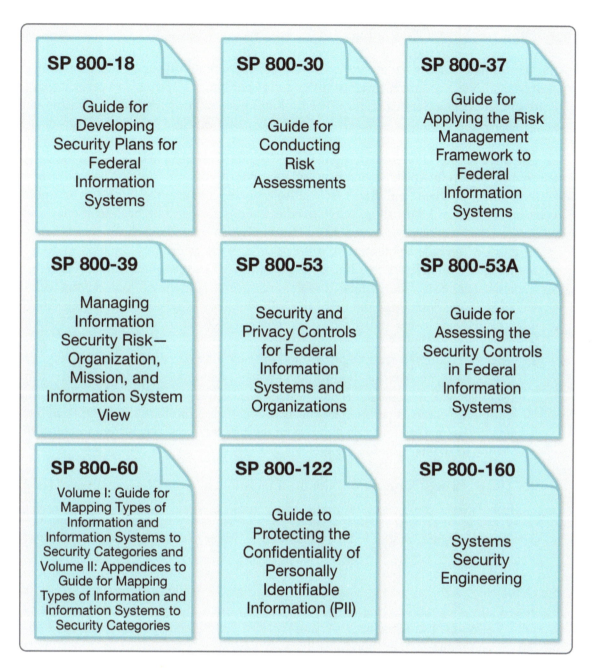

Figure 9: Initial Roadmap for Developing Complementary Federal Guidance for Privacy Engineering and Risk Management

In addition, working collaboratively, NIST will identify other work products that can help agencies to better understand the roles, tasks, and technical processes in privacy engineering and risk management. This guidance should shed light on how privacy engineering objectives and a privacy risk model can complement the FIPPs and PIAs to continually improve privacy programs. Over time, NIST anticipates that agencies will have a complete set of tools to enable privacy to achieve parity with other considerations in agencies' enterprise risk management processes.

Appendix A: NIST Development Process

In order to understand what activities and concepts are required for effective privacy engineering, NIST sought the perspectives and experiences of privacy experts across a variety of sectors in an open and transparent process, including hosting workshops, soliciting public comments, and engaging stakeholders in outreach activities in a broad range of settings.

As called for in the NIST Roadmap for Improving Critical Infrastructure Cybersecurity, NIST held public events in April, September, and October of 2014.[78] The first two were in Gaithersburg, Maryland, and San Jose, California, respectively; the third was an interactive webcast. At the April workshop, NIST led discussions focusing on organizational privacy challenges. The workshop also evaluated risk models in other disciplines—such as cybersecurity—and their potential to inform similar work in privacy. In addition to the 240 stakeholders that attended the workshop in person, over 100 people attended via webcast. These participants spanned a wide variety of sectors representing the legal, policy, and technical aspects of privacy. Attendees identified the following key issues, which helped NIST focus its attention on the development of privacy engineering objectives and a risk model:

1. There is a communication gap around privacy between the legal and policy, design and engineering, and product and project management teams that increases the difficulty for organizations to manage privacy concerns effectively, understand risks and implement mitigating controls before harm occurs. A contributing factor is the lack of a common vocabulary and set of tools that can be used to build consistent requirements and technical standards across agencies.

2. There is a need for more development tools that measure the effectiveness of privacy practices.

3. Risk management should be a fundamental driver of an agency's approach to privacy.

The second workshop had over 130 in-person attendees and an additional 500 participants during the October 5th webcast. At this workshop and during the webcast, participants reviewed and discussed NIST's initial draft of the privacy engineering objectives and a system privacy risk model.[79] Following the September workshop, NIST held an open comment period on these objectives and requested additional feedback. Numerous organizations responded to the call for comments, including major technology companies, civil society organizations, trade associations, and federal agencies.[80]

In May 2015, NIST released the draft of this report for a public comment period.[81] In August, over 40 private, public, academic, and other organizations and individuals submitted comments that contributed to this final report. This publication refines the version of the framework

---

[78] "NIST Privacy Engineering Workshop," *supra* note 54.
[79] The NIST workshop "Privacy Engineering Objectives and Risk Model Discussion Draft" is *available at* https://www.nist.gov/sites/default/files/documents/itl/csd/nist_privacy_engr_objectives_risk_model_discussion_draft.pdf.
[80] Draft NISTIR 8062 "Privacy Risk Management for Federal Information Systems" (MAY 2015), *available at* http://csrc.nist.gov/publications/drafts/nistir-8062/nistir_8062_draft.pdf.
[81] Ibid.

originally presented in the September 2014 workshop and reflects feedback received in workshop discussions, public comments and outreach.

NIST has conducted other outreach efforts, spreading awareness about privacy engineering while engaging stakeholders across the fields of privacy and cybersecurity. This includes formal presentations to key federal stakeholders, including the privacy committee of the U.S. Government's Chief Information Officers Council, the National Privacy Research Forum of the Networking and Information Technology Research and Development (more commonly known as NITRD) program, and the NIST Information Security and Privacy Advisory Board (ISPAB). NIST has presented to numerous academic institutions, federal agencies, trade associations and other stakeholders from private industry, and advocacy organizations. Through this outreach, NIST has received feedback from a wide array of stakeholders, better informing the development of the concepts in this document.

Appendix B: Glossary

Context: The circumstances surrounding the system's processing of PII.

Data Actions: System operations that process PII.

Disassociability: Enabling the processing of PII or events without association to individuals or devices beyond the operational requirements of the system.

Manageability: Providing the capability for granular administration of PII including alteration, deletion, and selective disclosure.

Personally Identifiable Information (PII): Information that can be used to distinguish or trace an individual's identity, either alone or when combined with other information that is linked or linkable to a specific individual.[82]

Predictability: Enabling of reliable assumptions by individuals, owners, and operators about PII and its processing by a system.

Privacy control: The administrative, technical, and physical safeguards employed within an agency to ensure compliance with applicable privacy requirements and manage privacy risks.[83]

Privacy engineering: A specialty discipline of systems engineering focused on achieving freedom from conditions that can create problems for individuals with unacceptable consequences that arise from the system as it processes PII.[84]

Problematic Data Action: A data action that causes an adverse effect, or problem, for individuals.

Processing: Operation or set of operations performed upon PII that can include, but is not limited to, the collection, retention, logging, generation, transformation, use, disclosure, transfer, and disposal of PII.[85]

Risk: A measure of the extent to which an entity or individual is threatened by a potential circumstance or event, and typically is a function of: (i) the adverse impact that would arise if the circumstance or event occurs; and (ii) the likelihood of occurrence.[86]

Senior Agency Official for Privacy: The senior official, designated by the head of each agency, who has agency-wide responsibility for privacy, including implementation of privacy protections; compliance with Federal laws, regulations, and policies relating to privacy;

---

[82] "Circular A-130," *supra* note 4 at p. 33.
[83] Id. at p. 34.
[84] See *supra* note 26 for considerations about the comprehensiveness of the term "PII" and the implications for privacy engineering in cyber-physical systems. In addition, for a related discussion about the definition of systems security engineering see "NIST SP 800-160," *supra* note 1, at p. 2.
[85] See "ISO/IEC 29100:2011(E)," *supra* note 25 for a related definition.
[86] "NIST SP 800-30 Rev1," *supra* note 44 at p. 8-13.

management of privacy risks at the agency; and a central policy-making role in the agency's development and evaluation of legislative, regulatory, and other policy proposals.

System: Combination of interacting elements organized to achieve one or more stated purposes.[87]

Systems Engineering:

Interdisciplinary approach governing the total technical and managerial effort required to transform a set of stakeholder needs, expectations, and constraints into a solution and to support that solution throughout its life.[88]

An engineering discipline whose responsibility is creating and executing an interdisciplinary process to ensure that the customer and all other stakeholder needs are satisfied in a high-quality, trustworthy, cost-efficient, and schedule-compliant manner throughout a system's entire life cycle.[89]

System privacy requirement: System requirements that have privacy relevance. System privacy requirements define the protection capabilities provided by the system, the performance and behavioral characteristics exhibited by the system, and the evidence used to determine that the system privacy requirements have been satisfied.

> *Note:* Each system privacy requirement is expressed in a manner that makes verification possible via analysis, observation, test, inspection, measurement, or other defined and achievable means.

> *Note*: This definition is derived from NIST SP 800-160.

Trustworthiness: Worthy of being trusted to fulfill whatever critical requirements may be needed for a particular component, subsystem, system, network, application, mission, enterprise, or other entity.

> *Note:* From a privacy perspective, a trustworthy system is a system that meets specific privacy requirements in addition to meeting other critical requirements.

> *Note*: This definition is derived from Neumann04, as referenced in NIST SP 800-160.

---

[87] "ISO/IEC/IEEE 15288," *supra* note 40.

[88] ISO/IEC/IEEE 24765, "Systems and software engineering – Vocabulary" (DEC 2010), *available at* http://www.iso.org/iso/catalogue_detail.htm?csnumber=50518.

[89] "What Is Systems Engineering," INCOSE, *available at* http://www.incose.org/AboutSE/WhatIsSE.

Appendix C: Acronyms

Acronyms and abbreviations used in this paper are defined below.

CIA   confidentiality, integrity, availability

DoT   Department of Transportation

FIPPs   Fair Information Practice Principles

ISO   International Organization for Standardization

IT   information technology

ITL   Information Technology Laboratory

NIST   National Institute of Standards and Technology

NITRD   Networking and Information Technology Research and Development

OASIS   Organization for the Advancement of Structured Information Standards

OMB   Office of Management and Budget

PIA   privacy impact assessment

PII   personally identifiable information

PMI   Precision Medicine Initiative

RMF   Risk Management Framework

UAS   Unmanned Aerial Systems

Appendix D: References

LEGISLATION

1. Federal Information Security Management Act of 2014, December 2014, https://www.gpo.gov/fdsys/pkg/USCODE-2015-title44/pdf/USCODE-2015-title44-chap35-subchapII-sec3552.pdf.

2. Privacy Act of 1974 (P.L. 107-56), December 1974, https://www.gpo.gov/fdsys/pkg/USCODE-2012-title5/pdf/USCODE-2012-title5-partI-chap5-subchapII-sec552a.pdf.

3. E-Government Act of 2002, 44 U.S.C. §101, December 2002, https://www.gpo.gov/fdsys/pkg/PLAW-107publ347/pdf/PLAW-107publ347.pdf.

4. Children's Online Privacy Protection Act, 15 U.S.C. §§ 6501–6506, October 1998, https://www.law.cornell.edu/uscode/text/15/chapter-91.

POLICIES, DIRECTIVES, REGULATIONS, AND MEMORANDA

5. Department of Health, Education, and Welfare, Secretary's Advisory Committee on Automated Personal Data Systems, *Records Computers and the Rights of Citizens*, June 1973, https://www.justice.gov/opcl/docs/rec-com-rights.pdf.

4. Federal Aviation Administration, *System Safety Process Steps*, January 2005, https://www.faa.gov/regulations_policies/handbooks_manuals/aviation/risk_management/media/ssprocdscrp.pdf.

5. Government Accountability Office, Report to Congressional Requesters, *High-Risk Series: An Update*, February 2015, http://www.gao.gov/assets/670/668415.pdf.

6. Government Accountability Office, Report to Congressional Requesters, *Actions Needed to Address Weaknesses in Information Security and Privacy Controls*, September 2014, http://www.gao.gov/assets/670/665840.pdf.

7. OMB, Executive Office of the President, Memorandum M-03-22, *OMB Guidance for Implementing the Privacy Provisions of the E-Government Act of 2002*, September 2003, https://www.whitehouse.gov/omb/memoranda_m03-22.

8. OMB, Executive Office of the President, Memorandum M-05-08, *Designation of Senior Agency Officials for Privacy*, February 2005, https://www.whitehouse.gov/sites/default/files/omb/assets/omb/memoranda/fy2005/m05-08.pdf.

9. OMB, Executive Office of the President, Memorandum M-10-22, *Guidance for Online Use of Web Measurement and Customization Technologies*, June 2010, https://www.whitehouse.gov/sites/default/files/omb/assets/memoranda_2010/m10-22.pdf.

31

10. OMB, Executive Office of the President, Memorandum M-10-23, *Guidance for Agency Use of Third-Party Websites and Applications*, June 2010, https://www.whitehouse.gov/sites/default/files/omb/assets/memoranda_2010/m10-23.pdf.

11. OMB, Executive Office of the President, Memorandum M-16-17, Circular A-123, *Management's Responsibility for Enterprise Risk Management and Internal Control*, July 2016, https://www.whitehouse.gov/sites/default/files/omb/memoranda/2016/m-16-17.pdf.

12. OMB, Executive Office of the President, *Model Privacy Impact Assessment for Agency Use of Third-Party Websites and Applications*, December 2011, https://www.whitehouse.gov/sites/default/files/omb/inforeg/info_policy/model-pia-agency-use-third-party-websites-and-applications.pdf.

13. The White House, *Administration Discussion Draft: Consumer Privacy Bill of Rights Act*, February 2015, https://www.whitehouse.gov/sites/default/files/omb/legislative/letters/cpbr-act-of-2015-discussion-draft.pdf.

14. The White House, Executive Office of the President, *Big Data: A Report on Algorithmic Systems, Opportunity, and Civil Rights*, May 2016, https://www.whitehouse.gov/sites/default/files/microsites/ostp/2016_0504_data_discrimination.pdf.

15. The White House, Circular A-130, *Managing Federal Information as a Strategic Resource*, July 2016, https://www.whitehouse.gov/sites/default/files/omb/assets/OMB/circulars/a130/a130revised.pdf.

16. The White House, Executive Office of the President, *National Privacy Research Strategy*, June 2016, https://www.whitehouse.gov/sites/default/files/nprs_nstc_review_final.pdf.

17. The White House, Executive Office of the President, *National Strategy For Trusted Identities In Cyberspace: Enhancing Online Choice, Efficiency, Security, and Privacy*, April 2011, https://www.whitehouse.gov/sites/default/files/rss_viewer/NSTICstrategy_041511.pdf.

18. The White House, *Presidential Memorandum: Promoting Economic Competitiveness While Safeguarding Privacy, Civil Rights, and Civil Liberties in Domestic Use of Unmanned Aircraft Systems*, February 2015, https://www.whitehouse.gov/the-press-office/2015/02/15/presidential-memorandum-promoting-economic-competitiveness-while-safegua.

19. The White House, *The Precision Medicine Initiative*, https://www.whitehouse.gov/precision-medicine.

STANDARDS

20. National Institute of Standards and Technology, Federal Information Processing Standards Publication 199, *Standards for Security Categorization of Federal Information and Information Systems*, February 2004, http://csrc.nist.gov/publications/fips/fips199/FIPS-PUB-199-final.pdf.

21. ISO/IEC/IEEE 15288, *Systems and software engineering—System life cycle processes,* May 2015, http://www.iso.org/iso/catalogue_detail?csnumber=63711.

22. ISO/IEC/IEEE 24765, *Systems and software engineering—Vocabulary*, December 2010, http://www.iso.org/iso/catalogue_detail.htm?csnumber=50518.

23. ISO/IEC 29100:2011(E), *Information technology—Security techniques—Privacy framework*, December 2011, http://standards.iso.org/ittf/PubliclyAvailableStandards/c045123_ISO_IEC_29100_2011.zip.

GUIDELINES, INTERAGENCY REPORTS, INTERNAL REPORTS, AND WHITE PAPERS

1. National Institute of Standards and Technology, *Framework for Improving Critical Infrastructure Cybersecurity*, February 2014, https://www.nist.gov/sites/default/files/documents/cyberframework/cybersecurity-framework-021214.pdf.

2. National Institute of Standards and Technology, *Privacy-Enhanced Identity Brokers*, October 2015, https://nccoe.nist.gov/sites/default/files/library/project-descriptions/privacy-enhanced-identity-brokers-project-description-draft.pdf.

3. National Institute of Standards and Technology, *Roadmap for Improving Critical Infrastructure Cybersecurity*, February 2014, https://www.nist.gov/sites/default/files/documents/cyberframework/roadmap-021214.pdf.

4. National Institute of Standards and Technology, Special Publication 800-18 Revision 1, *Guide for Developing Security Plans for Federal Information Systems*, February 2006, http://dx.doi.org/10.6028/NIST.SP.800-18r1.

5. National Institute of Standards and Technology, Special Publication 800-30 Revision 1, *Guide for Conducting Risk Assessments*, September 2012, https://doi.org/10.6028/NIST.SP.800-30r1.

6. National Institute of Standards and Technology, Special Publication 800-37 Revision 1, *Guide for Applying the Risk Management Framework to Federal Information Systems: A Security Life Cycle Approach*, February 2010 (updated June 5, 2014), https://doi.org/10.6028/NIST.SP.800-37r1.

7. National Institute of Standards and Technology, Special Publication 800-39, *Managing Information Security Risk: Organization, Mission, and Information System View*, March 2011, https://doi.org/10.6028/NIST.SP.800-39.

8. National Institute of Standards and Technology, Special Publication 800-53 Revision 4, *Security and Privacy Controls for Federal Information Systems and Organizations*, April 2013 (updated January 22, 2015), https://doi.org/10.6028/NIST.SP.800-53r4.

9. National Institute of Standards and Technology, Special Publication 800-53A Revision 4, *Assessing Security and Privacy Controls in Federal Information Systems and Organizations*, December 2014 (updated December 18, 2014), http://dx.doi.org/10.6028/NIST.SP.800-53Ar4.

10. National Institute of Standards and Technology, Special Publication 800-60, Volume 1, Revision 1, *Guide for Mapping Types of Information and Information Systems to Security Categories*, August 2008, http://dx.doi.org/10.6028/NIST.SP.800-60v1r1; National Institute of Standards and Technology Special Publication 800-60, Volume II, Revision 1, *Appendices to Guide for Mapping Types of Information and Information Systems to Security Categories*, August 2008, http://dx.doi.org/10.6028/NIST.SP.800-60v2r1.

11. National Institute of Standards and Technology, Special Publication 800-122, *Guide to Protecting the Confidentiality of Personally Identifiable Information (PII)*, April 2010, https://doi.org/10.6028/NIST.SP.800-122.

12. National Institute of Standards and Technology, Special Publication 800-160, *Systems Security Engineering: Considerations for a Multidisciplinary Approach in the Engineering of Trustworthy Secure Systems*, November 2016, https://doi.org/10.6028/NIST.SP.800-160.

13. National Institute of Standards and Technology, Special Publication 800-175A, *Guideline for Using Cryptographic Standards in the Federal Government: Directives, Mandates and Policies*, August 2016, https://doi.org/10.6028/NIST.SP.800-175A; National Institute of Standards and Technology Special Publication 800-175B, *Guideline for Using Cryptographic Standards in the Federal Government: Cryptographic Mechanisms*, August 2016, https://doi.org/10.6028/NIST.SP.800-175B.

14. National Institute of Standards and Technology, Special Publication 800-188 (2nd Draft), *De-Identifying Government Datasets*, December 2016, http://csrc.nist.gov/publications/drafts/800-188/sp800_188_draft2.pdf.

15. National Institute of Standards and Technology, Interagency Report 7628 Revision 1, *Guidelines for Smart Grid Cybersecurity: Volume 2 – Privacy and the Smart Grid*, September 2014, https://doi.org/10.6028/NIST.IR.7628r1.

16. National Institute of Standards and Technology, Interagency Report 8053, *De-Identification of Personal Information*, October 2015, https://doi.org/10.6028/NIST.IR.8053.

17. National Institute of Standards and Technology, Internal Report 8062 (Draft), *Privacy Risk Management for Federal Information Systems*, May 2015, http://csrc.nist.gov/publications/drafts/nistir-8062/nistir_8062_draft.pdf.

18. National Institute of Standards and Technology, Internal Report 8112 (Draft), *Attribute Metadata,* August 2016, http://csrc.nist.gov/publications/drafts/nistir-8112/nistir_8112_draft.pdf.

19. National Institute of Standards and Technology, Special Publication 1500-4, *NIST Big Data Interoperability Framework: Volume 4, Security and Privacy*, September 2015, https://doi.org/10.6028/NIST.SP.1500-4.

Appendix E: Examples of Non Data Breach Privacy Concerns

This appendix provides examples of systems that demonstrate various types of privacy concerns apart from data breaches. These concerns relate to the ways in which the systems are processing PII and the effects such processing can have on people.

1. Cyber-Physical Systems

Cyber-physical systems, particularly as amplified by big data, can raise a variety of privacy concerns, including "intentional or implicit biases" which can be reflected in systems that cross the boundaries between cyberspace and the physical world—like public safety and predictive policing systems.[90] Because cyber-physical systems extend systems into the physical realm, they raise concerns not just about their processing of PII, but also about their effect on people's physical activity or autonomy. Working with Smart Grid technology, NIST and its partners in the energy sector have noted public concern about smart meters due to the ability of these meters to collect, record, and distribute high-resolution information about household electrical use. Such information could be used, for example, to learn when a person or group of people were in a house and what appliances they were using. NIST concluded: "While many of the types of data items accessible through the smart grid are not new, there is now the possibility that other parties, entities or individuals will have access to those data items; and there are now many new uses for and ways to analyze the collected data, which may raise substantial privacy concerns."[91]

Cities are also seeking to use cyber-physical systems with powerful sensor technology to improve public services and infrastructure. This collection of information presents privacy challenges in transportation and urban operations, including concerns about surveillance and inaccurate or inappropriate determinations of guilt (such as with red-light traffic cameras).[92] The proliferation of advanced camera and sensor technology may even "[threaten] to upset the balance of power between city governments and city residents, and to destroy the sense of privacy and urban anonymity that has defined urban life over the past century."[93]

---

[90] "Big Data: A Report on Algorithmic Systems, Opportunity, and Civil Rights," Executive Office of the President, The White House (MAY 2016) at p. 6, *available at* https://www.whitehouse.gov/sites/default/files/microsites/ostp/2016_0504_data_discrimination.pdf, [hereinafter known as "Big Data"];
the "Framework for Cyber-Physical Systems, Release 1.0" Cyber Physical Systems Public Working Group (2016) at p. 74, *available at* https://s3.amazonaws.com/nist-sgcps/cpspwg/files/pwgglobal/CPS_PWG_Framework_for_Cyber_Physical_Systems_Release_1_0Final.pdf; Special Publication 1500-4, "NIST Big Data Interoperability Framework: Volume 4, Security and Privacy" (APRIL 2015), *available at* https://doi.org/10.6028/NIST.SP.1500-4.

[91] "NISTIR 7628 Rev1," *supra* note 5.

[92] Luke Broadwater, "City Surveillance Camera System to Expand," Baltimore Sun (JULY 2012), *available at* http://articles.baltimoresun.com/2012-07-21/news/bs-md-ci-private-cameras-20120721_1_security-cameras-crime-cameras-citiwatch-system. See also Jay Stanley, "Extreme Traffic Enforcement," American Civil Liberties Union (MAY 2012), *available at* https://www.aclu.org/blog/extreme-traffic-enforcement; and Phineas Baxandall, "New Report Outlines Problems with Red-Light and Speed Cameras," The Federation of Public Research Interest Groups (OCT 2011), *available at* http://www.uspirg.org/trafficcamreport.

[93] Kelsey Finch and Omer Tene, "Welcome to the Metropticon: Protecting Privacy in a Hyperconnected Town," Fordham Urban L. J., volume 41 at p. 1581, 1595 (2015), *available at* http://ir.lawnet.fordham.edu/cgi/viewcontent.cgi?article=2549&context=ulj.

The U.S. Department of Transportation (DoT) has broadly cataloged some of these concerns in its work on connected vehicles, and is using its Smart Cities Challenge program to explore technical and policy frameworks to address emergent privacy risks.[94] The DoT has stated "The Internet of Things is a world where anything with intelligence will have an online presence, generating rich, contextual data that could be put to uses currently perhaps unimagined. The value of these possibilities rests on systems that measure, track, and analyze more about our world than ever before. The new volume and variety of data creates new privacy risks."[95] For example, law enforcement may be able to remotely pull over automated vehicles with passengers inside or smart city technologies can be used to alter or influence people's behavior such as where or how they move through the city.[96]

Cyber-physical systems are being utilized to improve many security operations, such as the Transportation Security Administration's initial deployment of Advanced Imaging Technologies, more colloquially known as "body scanners." These systems—designed to detect prohibited items carried by individuals into secure areas of airports—raised public concern about individuals' reasonable expectation of privacy under their clothing.[97] The Department of Homeland Security's PIA focused predominantly on how this non-breach concern was addressed.[98]

Privacy concerns related to personal spaces and activities have been of particular note in the rapid proliferation of Unmanned Aerial Systems. Small drones equipped with high-resolution cameras can potentially draw in a large amount of data not related to their originally intended purpose: "On some drones, operators can track up to 65 different targets across a distance of 65 square miles. Drones may also carry infrared cameras, heat sensors, GPS, sensors that detect movement, and automated license plate readers. In the near future these cameras may include facial recognition technology that would make it possible to remotely identify individuals in parks, schools, and at political gatherings."[99] The White House and many federal agencies have raised concerns that drone-based data collection, retention, or dissemination could result in violations of the First Amendment or lead to discriminatory actions that jeopardize individuals' civil rights and liberties.[100] Privacy advocates have highlighted that drones create the capacity for

---

[94] "Privacy In a Connected Vehicle Environment," Department of Transportation (AUG 2014) at slide 9, http://www.its.dot.gov/itspac/Dec2014/ITSPAC_PrivacyCVBriefing.pdf. See also, for more information, "Questions and Answers for the Beyond Traffic Smart City Challenge," *available at* https://www.transportation.gov/smartcity/q-and-a.

[95] "The Smart/Connected City and Its Implications for Connected Transportation," Department of Transportation (OCT 2014) at chapter 3.1.4, *available at* http://www.its.dot.gov/itspac/Dec2014/Smart_Connected_City_FINAL_111314.pdf.

[96] "Self-Driving Cars," and "Security, Privacy, Governance Concerns About Smart City Technologies Grow," *supra* note 26.

[97] Timothy D. Sparapani, Statement Before the Senate Committee on Commerce, Science, and Technology, Regarding the US TSA's Physical Screening of Airline Passengers and Related Cargo Screening, "Principles for Evaluating Physical Screening Techniques and Technologies Consistent with Constitutional Norms," American Civil Liberties Union Legislative Counsel (APR 2006), *available at* https://www.aclu.org/other/statement-timothy-d-sparapani-aclu-legislative-counsel-hearing-regarding-us-transportation.

[98] "Privacy Impact Assessment Update for TSA Advanced Imaging Technology," Department of Homeland Security (DEC 2015), *available at* https://www.dhs.gov/sites/default/files/publications/privacy-tsa-pia-32-d-ait.pdf.

[99] "Domestic Unmanned Aerial Vehicles (UAVs) and Drones," Electronic Privacy Information Center, https://epic.org/privacy/drones/.

[100] "Presidential Memorandum: Promoting Economic Competitiveness While Safeguarding Privacy, Civil Rights, and Civil Liberties in Domestic Use of Unmanned Aircraft Systems," The White House (FEB 2015), *available at* https://www.whitehouse.gov/the-press-office/2015/02/15/presidential-memorandum-promoting-economic-competitiveness-while-safegua; "U.S. Department of Homeland Security Best Practices for Protecting Privacy, Civil Rights & Civil Liberties In Unmanned Aircraft Systems Programs," U.S. Department of Homeland Security Privacy, Civil Rights & Civil Liberties

privacy risks "even in traditionally protected private spaces like [individuals'] homes. Continuous and persistent surveillance represents one of the most privacy invasive potential uses of UAS, and one that many Americans most fear drones will be used for."[101]

2. Personal Health Information

A number of initiatives in the healthcare space have been faced with privacy concerns that threaten participation in potentially valuable public research and services. A recent NIH report described how potential contributors to large-scale health studies have a number of privacy concerns outside of data theft or security issues: "For those who consent to take part in the study, most if not all instances of the sharing of participants' data by the biobank should be viewed as acceptable. It is, however, possible to envision instances of data sharing or release that could be viewed by a participant as a violation of privacy. Participants may misunderstand or underestimate the extent to which they have consented to share their data and subsequently view some legitimate data sharing as a loss of privacy."[102]

Concerns about individuals' privacy and the impact it can have on public health initiatives prompted the White House to develop "Privacy and Trust" principles for its PMI that are distinct from the information safeguards in its "Data Security Policy Principles and Framework."[103] The Privacy and Trust principles describe the importance of preventing data inaccuracies and unnecessary re-identification, and the importance of privacy to preserving public trust in the Initiative. As part of the PMI, the Veteran's Administration's PIA for its Genomic Information System for Integrated Science research program cataloged specific risks, including, but not limited to:

- "The re-identification of information linked to a specific individual, notwithstanding representations that a participant's information would be anonymous or not identifiable...
- Participants misunderstand or underestimate the extent to which they have consented to share their data...
- The perception of a loss of medical or other privacy leading to a change in behavior.
- Embarrassment or stigma associated with certain information should that information be released or tied to the individual...
- Perceived or real risks that information could be used to discriminate against a group of individuals in different contexts such as employment or insurance discrimination...

Unmanned Aircraft Systems Working Group (DEC 2015), *available at* https://www.dhs.gov/sites/default/files/publications/UAS%20Best%20Practices.pdf; and "Department of Justice Policy Guidance1 Domestic Use of Unmanned Aircraft Systems (UAS)," U.S. Department of Justice, *available at* https://www.justice.gov/file/441266/download.

[101] "Letter from Privacy Groups to Participants in the NTIA Multi-Stakeholder Process on Unmanned Aircraft Systems" (2016), *available at* https://www.accessnow.org/cms/assets/uploads/2016/05/Letter-on-UAS-best-practices-FINAL-5-2016.pdf.

[102] That same study from NIH found 79% of respondents had concerns about their privacy when considering participating in a health study. Over half (56%) were concerned about the researchers' access to their information—illustrating fundamental concerns about privacy even during access by authorized parties. The full report is *available at* http://www.ncbi.nlm.nih.gov/pmc/articles/PMC2775831/pdf/main.pdf.

[103] "The Precision Medicine Initiative," *supra* note 6; "Precision Medicine Initiative: Data Security Policy Principles and Framework," The White House (MAY 2016), *available at* https://www.whitehouse.gov/sites/whitehouse.gov/files/documents/PMI_Security_Principles_Framework_v2.pdf.

- Information is accessed by law enforcement for reasons beyond research...”[104]

Outside of the research area, the Healthcare.gov website implemented third-party analytics add-ons and tools that could view information about site visitors including age, pregnancy, parental status, zip code, state, and income.[105] Advocates testified that “Consumers in disadvantaged communities face more potential for harm—such as being profiled in data banks as “Rural and Barely Making It,” “Ethnic Second-City Strugglers,” and “Retiring on Empty: Singles.,” categories which a recent Senate Commerce Committee report found. These characterizations may then prompt advertising of the type of subprime mortgage loans and other predatory lending that perpetuates the cycle of poverty.”[106] Still others have raised privacy concerns about law enforcement access to repositories of health information.[107]

3. Big Data and Analytical Systems

A recent White House report described how advances in large-scale data analytics have come with privacy concerns, including creating unintended bias or discrimination in systems that determine edibility for goods, services, and employment opportunities.[108] The U.S. Department of Homeland Security’s (DHS) Automated Targeting System (ATS) is a decision support tool that compares traveler, cargo, and conveyance information against law enforcement, intelligence, and other enforcement data using risk-based targeting scenarios and assessments.[109] DHS proposed enhancements to the ATS in 2006 that would allow the system to ingest public social media postings and “Suspicious Activity Reports” (SARs) to improve the intelligence of the system.[110] Privacy and civil liberties advocates raised concerns that using social media postings and opaque SARs (intelligence reports of individuals’ behavior ranging from terrorist activities to political protests) for situational awareness would be “the establishment of a massive black box with detailed profiles, ratings, and targeting rules concerning US citizens that will be widely

---

[104] “GENESIS,” *supra* note 7.

[105] Cooper Quintin, “HealthCare.gov Sends Personal Data to Dozens of Tracking Websites,” Electronic Frontier Foundation (JAN 2015), *available at* https://www.eff.org/deeplinks/2015/01/healthcare.gov-sends-personal-data.

[106] Statement of Michelle Kathleen De Mooy, Statement Before the United States House of Representatives Committee on Science, Space, and Technology, Subcommittee on Research and Technology, Subcommittee on Oversight, “Can Americans Trust the Privacy and Security of Their Information on HealthCare.gov?” Center for Democracy & Technology (FEB 2015), *available at* https://cdt.org/files/2015/02/2015-02-11-Michelle-De-Mooy-House-Science-Committee-Hearing-on-HealthCaregov-FINAL.pdf.

[107] “Law Enforcement Investigators Demand Access To Private DNA Databases,” Associated Press (MARCH 2016), *available at* http://sanfrancisco.cbslocal.com/2016/03/26/law-enforcement-investigators-demand-private-dna-databases/.

[108] “Big Data,” *supra* note 90.

[109] DHS/CBP/PIA-006(d) “Automated Targeting System (ATS) Update: TSA-CBP Common Operating Picture Phase II,” Department of Homeland Security (AUG 2015), *available at* https://www.dhs.gov/publication/automated-targeting-system-ats-update.

[110] DHS-OPS-PIA-004 “Publicly Available Social Media Monitoring and Situational Awareness Initiative,” Department of Homeland Security (MAY 2015), *available at* https://www.dhs.gov/publication/dhs-ops-pia-004f-publicly-available-social-media-monitoring-and-situational-awareness. See also DHS/OPA/PIA-003 “Suspicious Activity Reports (SARs) Project,” Department of Homeland Security (NOV 2008*), available at* https://www.dhs.gov/publication/dhsopspia-003-suspicious-activity-reports-sars-project.

accessible across the federal government and may be used for a wide variety of agency activities but will not be available to the person about whom decisions will be made."[111]

In another example, the Customs and Border Patrol's (CBP) Electronic System for Travel Authorization (ESTA) collects information from travelers entering the United States in order to assess potential risks to national security and support the determination of an individuals' admissibility to the United States.[112] CBP proposed an addition to the system that would require individuals to submit their social media identifiers so their online activity could be analyzed for national security and admissibility concerns.[113] Many organizations and individuals raised concerns about privacy, including unanticipated revelations about individuals and their online connections and communities, the obligation to release potentially stigmatizing information about communities or individuals, distortion of incomplete information or information translated from other languages, and a broader potential "chilling effect" on individuals' free speech online.[114]

---

[111] "Comments of 30 organizations and 16 experts in privacy and technology urging the Department of Homeland Security to (a) suspend the 'Automated Targeting System' as applied to individuals, or in the alternative, (b) fully apply all privacy act safeguards to any person subject to the automated targeting system." Electronic Privacy Information Center (2006), *available at* https://epic.org/privacy/pdf/ats_comments.pdf.

[112] "Electronic System for Travel Authorization," U.S. Customs and Border Protection, *available at* https://esta.cbp.dhs.gov/esta/.

[113] The Federal Register, "Agency Information Collection Activities: Arrival and Departure Record (Forms I-94 and I-94W) and Electronic System for Travel Authorization," U.S. Customs and Border Protection (JUNE 2016), *available at* https://www.federalregister.gov/articles/2016/06/23/2016-14848/agency-information-collection-activities-arrival-and-departure-record-forms-i-94-and-i-94w-and#p-16.

[114] "Internet Association Comment on DHS Social Media Identifiers" (AUG 2016), *available at* https://www.regulations.gov/document?D=USCBP-2007-0102-0585; for additional similar concerns, see the ETSA public comment repository: https://www.regulations.gov/docketBrowser?rpp=50&so=DESC&sb=postedDate&po=0&dct=PS&D=USCBP-2007-0102.

Appendix F: The Fair Information Practice Principles (FIPPs)[115]

Access and Amendment: Agencies should provide individuals with appropriate access to PII and appropriate opportunity to correct or amend PII.

Accountability: Agencies should be accountable for complying with these principles and applicable privacy requirements, and should appropriately monitor, audit, and document compliance. Agencies should also clearly define the roles and responsibilities with respect to PII for all employees and contractors, and should provide appropriate training to all employees and contractors who have access to PII.

Authority: Agencies should only create, collect, use, process, store, maintain, disseminate, or disclose PII if they have authority to do so, and should identify this authority in the appropriate notice.[116]

Minimization: Agencies should only create, collect, use, process, store, maintain, disseminate, or disclose PII that is directly relevant and necessary to accomplish a legally authorized purpose, and should only maintain PII for as long as is necessary to accomplish the purpose.[117]

Quality and Integrity: Agencies should create, collect, use, process, store, maintain, disseminate, or disclose PII with such accuracy, relevance, timeliness, and completeness as is reasonably necessary to ensure fairness to the individual.

Individual Participation: Agencies should involve the individual in the process of using PII and, to the extent practicable, seek individual consent for the creation, collection, use, processing, storage, maintenance, dissemination, or disclosure of PII. Agencies should also establish procedures to receive and address individuals' privacy-related complaints and inquiries.

Purpose Specification and Use Limitation: Agencies should provide notice of the specific purpose for which PII is collected and should only use, process, store, maintain, disseminate, or disclose PII for a purpose that is explained in the notice and is compatible with the purpose for which the PII was collected, or that is otherwise legally authorized.

Security: Agencies should establish administrative, technical, and physical safeguards to protect PII commensurate with the risk and magnitude of the harm that would result from its unauthorized access, use, modification, loss, destruction, dissemination, or disclosure.

Transparency: Agencies should be transparent about information policies and practices with respect to PII, and should provide clear and accessible notice regarding creation, collection, use, processing, storage, maintenance, dissemination, and disclosure of PII.[118]

---

[115] "Circular A-130," *supra* note 4.

[116] The Authority principle is included as part of the "Purpose Specification" privacy control family in "NIST SP 800-53 Rev4," *supra* note 17. OMB is including Authority as a stand-alone principle in this Circular to emphasize the importance of identifying a specific authority for creating, collecting, using, processing, storing, maintaining, disseminating, or disclosing PII.

[117] In some versions of the FIPPs, the "minimization" principle is referred to under a different name (e.g., "collection limitation").

[118] In some versions of the FIPPs, the "transparency" principle is referred to under a different name, such as "openness."